BRYANT COLLEGE:
THE FIRST 125 YEARS

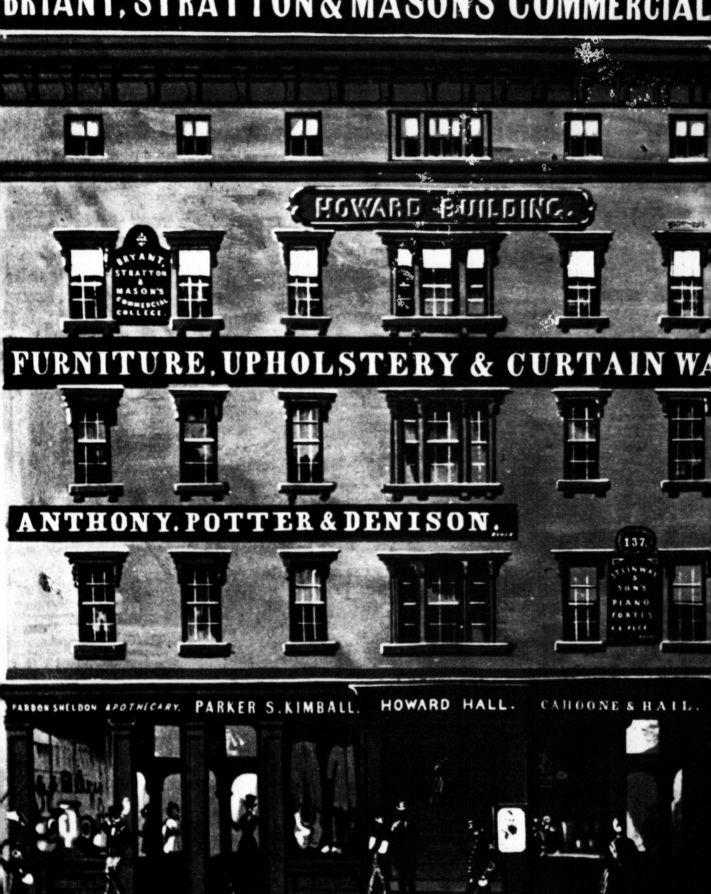

Bryant College
The First 125 Years

by Valerie Quinney

edited by Peter Mandel and Elizabeth O'Neil

SMITHFIELD, RHODE ISLAND • 1988

PHOTOGRAPHY RESEARCH: Carol Hagglund

PHOTOGRAPHY AND ILLUSTRATIONS: Bryant College Archives, Bob Aude, Fabian Bachrach, Denise Bastien, Matthew Brady, Providence Journal Company (by permission), Providence Public Library, Rhode Island Historical Society, Jeanne Richardson, William M. Rittase, Stephen Spencer, Jack Spratt, Stephen W. Whitney

Copyright by Bryant College, 1988

ISBN Number: 0-9619687-0-2

Library of Congress Catalog Card Number: 87-63603

CONTENTS

FROM THE BIRTH of the Bryant and Stratton National Business College through the current era of expansion on the Smithfield campus, *Bryant College: The First 125 Years* is the story of an institution that has grown and prospered far more rapidly than its founders could ever have imagined.

This is a book which will make Bryant come to life every time you pick it up. In a sense, it is the college's 125th anniversary record book, picturing the important people, places and events that have shaped the institution during its first century and a quarter.

Of all the projects that have evolved around Bryant's 125th anniversary, this Bryant history will have, perhaps, the most lasting significance. While speeches fade and special events blur into memories, a book such as this will endure as long as there are people who care about Bryant College.

As you share my pride in the college's rich traditions and colorful history, I trust that this volume will become part of your "permanent collection" of Bryant memorabilia.

WILLIAM T. O'HARA
President of Bryant College

Bryant and Stratton's National Business College

I N THE MID 1800s it was difficult for the ambitious young person to begin a career in business. As one observer remarked, "It was impossible to learn bookkeeping without getting into business and impossible to get into business without having learned book-keeping."[1] Two enterprising young midwesterners, Henry Bryant and Henry Stratton, decided that the answer was a business school. The traditional year-long apprenticeship in business delayed advancement, and apprenticeships were hard to obtain. A short, intensive training period in a business school would give the necessary preparation for a career.

Some educators in this country had offered instruction in business-related subjects early in the century and a few business schools had been established by mid-century. Stratton and Bryant figured that the demand for commercial education would greatly increase. In 1853, they secured a penmanship teacher, James Lusk, as partner and backer, and the three opened Bryant, Stratton and Lusk College in Cleveland. Within a few months Lusk had dropped out of the business venture, but Bryant and Stratton were dreaming of expanding and building a chain of colleges all over the country. Within two years, they set up a business school in Buffalo, New York, and persuaded Henry Bryant's brother, John, a medical doctor, to manage the Buffalo college for them. This was the first in the chain; during the next ten years they founded an additional eighteen colleges. Bryant and Stratton gave competitors in their chosen cities ruthless competition and sometimes bought them out. The idea for a chain of schools was not exclusively theirs but they had the most success with it.

The Civil War gave Bryant and Stratton's business schools an extra impetus for growth: veterans wanted to invest their mustering-out pay in an enterprise that would end in a job. In the late 1860s, they flocked to these colleges.[2] Bryant and Stratton used the profits to found more colleges and ended up with forty-four altogether. Among these was the Bryant and Stratton National Business College in Providence, Rhode Island. Founded in 1863, the school's astounding success provides an interesting ancestral history to the present Bryant College.

To build their educational empire, Henry Bryant and Henry Stratton took advantage of a combination of historical events and human

Soldiers returned from the Civil War with "mustering out" pay in their pockets and a desire to enter the workforce as quickly as possible. For $50 they could learn business skills in a matter of months at the Bryant and Stratton National Business College.

talents. The expansion of business enterprises in this country during the second half of the nineteenth century created unprecedented job opportunities for office workers.[3] In this period, offices became larger so that it was no longer possible for the owner to supervise every person in the office including his clerk-apprentices. Consequently, there were just not enough apprenticeships to meet the demand for competent clerks. Bryant and Stratton correctly surmised that young men would need a business education for the jobs opening up in great numbers.

Both Henry Bryant and Henry Stratton were often described as being full of energy and hope.[4] In terms of organizing and teaching abilities, the two Henrys complemented each other. Henry Bryant supervised the courses of study. Henry Stratton was the all-around business expert. Those who came in contact with Stratton were impressed by his sense of the importance of his mission and his belief in honest work.[5] And Bryant and Stratton were astute in recognizing talent in others. John Bryant remained president of the Buffalo institution until his death, but he also served as a consultant in the management of the other colleges in the chain and became known nationally for his leadership in the field of business education.[6] The two Henrys persuaded Platt R. Spencer, who had developed the famous Spencerian script, to teach writing for them.[7] His supervision of writing in the Bryant and Stratton colleges greatly enhanced their prestige. They also hired Silas Packard, who had excelled in grammar, mathematics, and penmanship as a student and had taught in several commercial colleges, to join them at the Buffalo college in 1856. Two years later Packard started the Bryant and Stratton College in New York City. For a time, he also managed the Chicago college. He had a keen mind, remarkable ability as an extemporaneous speaker, and a good sense of humor.[8] In the last quarter of the century, his leadership in business education led to his election to the presidency of a national educational association.

Henry Bryant (above) and Henry Stratton started their first business school in 1853 with James Lusk as penmanship teacher and financial backer. Good penmanship was an important business skill before the typewriter. Bryant and Stratton published their own practice ledgers and textbooks.

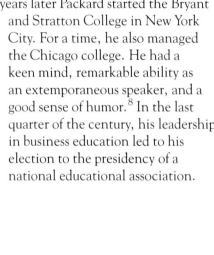

COMMISSION AND FORWARDING
RECEIVING BOOK.

BRYANT, STRATTON & CO'S
GREAT
CHAIN OF INTERNATIONAL

BUSINESS COLLEGES,

LOCATED AT

Henry Stratton found businessmen and educators in cities throughout the midwest to become partners in local branches of the Bryant and Stratton chain. At its peak there were forty-four branches.

Before 1890, business courses were rarely taught in traditional colleges or high schools, so business schools had a monopoly on this kind of education. However, there were few textbooks on business subjects. In the early days, business schools produced their own texts and the quality of the texts determined, more or less, the quality of the education.

Bryant and Stratton wanted the best. Packard prepared the texts on bookkeeping for all the colleges in their chain. His bookkeeping texts and the Packard manual on arithmetic became the leading books on these subjects. They were sold not only to the students in the chain's forty-four colleges but were also translated for use in business schools in Belgium and France.[9] Amos Dean, head of the Albany Law School, wrote the textbook on commercial law for the chain. The June 1903 issue of *Business Educator* commented on Bryant and Stratton's texts: "These works made the most complete series of publications for commercial schools that had been published and were important aids in broadening, deepening, and elevating Commercial Education."[10]

Marketing was also important in the success of the Bryant and Stratton colleges. Like other business schools, Bryant and Stratton prepared flyers with testimonials to the high quality of instruction and to the usefulness of the training. The flyers were handed out on the street. An advertising ploy Bryant and Stratton used was the "interchangeable scholarship": the tuition that students paid and the credit they received could be transferred to a Bryant and Stratton college in another city if the student wanted to move. Bryant and Stratton chose commercial buildings in the middle of business districts as locations for their colleges and spread banners across the front of the buildings advertising the presence and availability of a business education. Every city newspaper carried advertisements informing the public about the local Bryant and Stratton College.

Most important in their strategy was the recruitment of outstanding businessmen and lawyers to teach and to suggest improvements in the courses and methods of instruction.[11] Business people became interested in the school because they taught there. They had a stake in the school's success: they sent students to it and hired its graduates. Graduation ceremonies were open to the public, featuring well-known businessmen, educators, and politicians as keynote speakers.

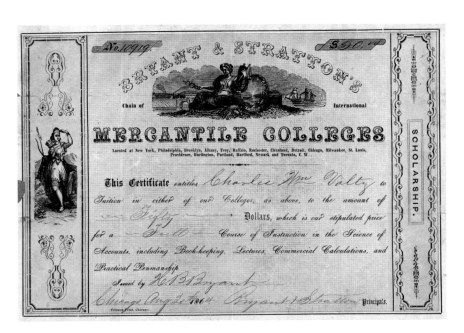

Bryant and Stratton developed a sophisticated marketing strategy. One of their advertising ploys was the "interchangeable scholarship." Tuition and academic credits could be transferred to any of the colleges in the chain.

As for admissions requirements, Bryant and Stratton colleges asked only that students have the ability to read English. Veterans returning from the Civil War and seeking education could rarely meet the stiff entrance requirements for liberal arts colleges, which included knowledge of Latin and Greek. Here was an institution that welcomed them simply because they could speak and read their own language. Here also was a program which did not require a commitment of four years but of only several months because a student progressed through the curriculum at his own pace (the usual practice in business schools). A student could enter at any time of the year and was ready for a job when he completed the work. Business schools usually assisted students in finding jobs, but Bryant and Stratton colleges paid special attention to this service.

Henry Stratton travelled all over the midwest and northeast seeking opportunities to expand. Among the sites Stratton chose, Providence, Rhode Island, a seaport surrounded by factories, seemed most likely to prove successful. Stratton found a local accountant, Ezra Mason, who was eager to manage the Providence college. The arrangement Bryant and Stratton set up with Mason was typical of the way they founded colleges in their chain. They wanted the principal to be a part-owner, not just a salaried employee. The agreement, signed in 1863 in New York by Henry Bryant, Henry Stratton, and Ezra Mason, had Mason promising to "devote his time and energies in advancing the interests of the College by teaching and looking after its interests generally." Bryant and Stratton agreed to "furnish the capital for opening the school and with the understanding that the said E. W. Mason shall refund to them one-half the amount so required that he shall become a half owner in the College."[12]

In Providence, the college started out on the third floor of the Lyceum Building (near the present Turk's Head Building) at 56 Westminster Street. The number of students grew so rapidly that additional rooms were rented in the Howard Building further down the block. Then the

The college's first home in 1863 was in the Lyceum Building on Westminster Street. Westminster (above) and neighboring Weybosset Street (below) were quite different in character from today's thoroughfares.

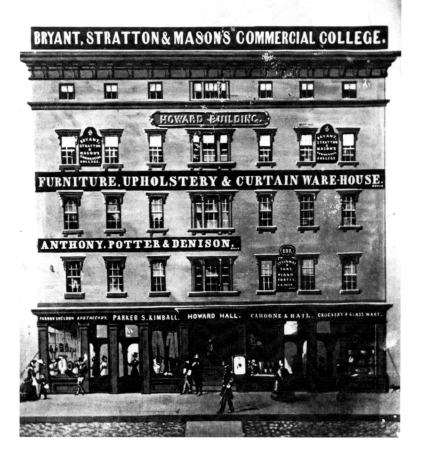

BRYANT, STRATTON & MASON'S COMMERCIAL COLLEGE.

HOWARD BUILDING.

FURNITURE, UPHOLSTERY & CURTAIN WARE-HOUSE.

ANTHONY, POTTER & DENISON.

Before long, the college needed additional space, and found it in the multi-faceted Howard Building.

college occupied the second and third floor of a building on the corner of Westminster and Clemence. The name "Bryant, Stratton and Mason National Business College" on the front of the building could be spotted immediately by any Civil War veteran who alighted from the train to seek his fortune in Providence, or by any aspiring boy who made his way along the streets to a menial job. There was even a small number of young women who saw the sign, took a flyer, and came knocking on the door.

Providence in the 1860s was a prosperous city with a cosmopolitan population. It was well known for the manufacture of woolens, jewelry, silverware, and hardware. Roughly half of its residents (56 percent) were of American parentage, but 44 percent had parents born in other countries—Ireland, England, Wales, Scotland, Germany, France, Portugal, and Italy.[13] People were reading the *Providence Journal,* started in 1830, and a brand new paper, the *Evening Bulletin.* The Rhode Island Hospital Trust Company had not yet been chartered, but Brown and Sharpe Factory was a growing concern. A. W. Sprague Manufacturing Company was the financial giant, however, and no one could foresee its ruin in the 1873 panic, or that it would drag down the Cranston Savings Bank and the Franklin Savings Bank. Brown University, chartered in 1764, was almost one hundred years old, but Providence College, the Rhode Island School of Design, and the University of Rhode Island were not yet glimpsed.

In Providence's Bryant and Stratton College, Ezra Mason wisely followed the chain's usual practices. He put out circulars in which the school's faculty and courses were described and the advantages of a business education extolled. He made sure graduates remained attached to the college by starting a club, the "What Cheer Lyceum," through which graduates and current students met to hear lectures and discuss current events. Musical entertainments, dances, and picnics also served to bring students and graduates together. One such social occasion, described as a "feast of reason" and "flow of soul," ended with a special ceremony. The students presented Mason with a tea set, manufactured by the Gorham and Brown Company. A former student, Charles Gorton of the Merchants' Bank, delivered the presentation speech, expressing "confidence in Mr. Mason as a successful teacher and esteem for him as a man." The students also gave a "beautiful amber cane, gold mounted and finely chased" to a favorite teacher, Charles Renter, an instructor in penmanship. The evening closed with a musical treat from the college band.[14]

The college moved from place to place in the Westminster Street area and, for a while, took up residence in the Burgess Building.

OPPOSITE:
Ezra Mason, the local partner in the Providence Bryant and Stratton College, sold his interest to William W. Warner in 1867. Warner added a wide range of courses and eventually changed the name to Warner's Polytechnic.

Mason cultivated contacts with businessmen. He made sure that all advertisements carried testimonials from businessmen who had hired graduates and from former students who had become successful in the business world. A typical one began:

> We, the undersigned, employers of students who have received instructions in Bryant, Stratton and Mason's Commercial College, cheerfully bear testimony to the success of the faculty of that institution in rendering the young men under their charge qualified for active business as soon as they have graduated.[15]

It was signed by heads of banks, manufacturers, and small businesses and by the postmaster of Rhode Island. Graduates also wrote testimonials for Mason, such as this one:

> We gladly attest the unswerving kindness and fidelity of the faculty towards all the students of the College, thereby rendering our course of study while under their instruction, at once pleasant and profitable.[16]

Mason described himself in college publications as Instructor in the Science of Accounts and Lecturer in the Theory and Practice of Business. His entire faculty, including himself, numbered eleven. Among them was one woman, Miss C. J. Arnold, who taught bookkeeping in the ladies' department.[17]

In 1864 the cost of the full program of studies was fifty dollars; this covered the usual length of time for a certificate—ten to fourteen weeks. Students bought their textbooks from the college: Bookkeeping $3.50, Commercial Law $3.50, Commercial Arithmetic $1.75, and notebooks $8.00. The total was a formidable sum for a student at the time, but once he had paid, the individual could stay in the school and take as many courses as he wished, for as long as he wished.[18]

The core program was called the Science of Accounts and included bookkeeping, business law, commercial arithmetic, practical penmanship, and business correspondence. Although students attended lectures, most of their learning was done in rooms adjacent to the lecture hall set up as a mock bank, mock store, and mock office. (As far as bookkeeping was concerned, emphasis on learning-by-doing was the usual practice in business schools in the mid-nineteenth century.)[19] Mason introduced samples representing the different goods for sale in the market so that students handled the actual products.[20] In their "store," they stocked goods, ordered, inventoried, shipped goods, involved themselves in retail sales, kept the accounts, and made out the payroll. They were given $1,000 in play money which they were charged to increase by investing. They later passed to the large office where they gained experience in such areas as insurance and then to the bank where they learned all the transactions which normally took place in a bank at the time. All forms which the students learned to deal with were those in current use.[21]

THE FIGHT FOR THE STANDARD

Our Superiority is Acknowledged !

The above specimen was written by me, as above stated, on the sixth day of April, 1870, before taking lessons at WARNER'S BRYANT & STRATTON BUSINESS COLLEGE.

CHARLES S. YOUNG.

The above specimen was written by me, on or about the 17th day of May, 1870, after receiving about Twenty lessons at WARNER'S BRYANT & STRATTON BUSINESS COLLEGE.

CHARLES S. YOUNG.

STATE OF RHODE ISLAND. }
Providence sc. }
PROVIDENCE, September 1st, 1871.
Personally appeared CHARLES S. YOUNG, and made oath that the above were specimens of his hand-writing at the time stated.
GEO. T. PAINE, Justice of the Peace.

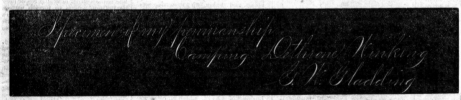

The above specimen was written by me after taking lessons three months at ——'s Commercial College, and before taking lessons at WARNER'S BRYANT & STRATTON COMMERCIAL COLLEGE.

GEORGE W. GLADDING.

The above specimen was written by me after receiving instruction in WARNER'S BRYANT & STRATTON COMMERCIAL COLLEGE about six weeks.

GEORGE W. GLADDING.

STATE OF RHODE ISLAND. }
Providence sc. }
PROVIDENCE, September 8th, 1871.
Personally appeared GEORGE W. GLADDING, and made oath that the above were specimens of his hand-writing as above stated.
GEORGE T. PAINE, Justice of the Peace.

The College is open Every School Day in the Year.

Evening Sessions commence September 4th, and continue until May.

CALL FOR A CIRCULAR.

WARNER'S BRYANT & STRATTON
NATIONAL
BUSINESS COLLEGE,

164 WESTMINSTER STREET, PROVIDENCE, R. I.

THE DESIGN

In publishing these

Specimens of Penmanship,

Is to show the SUPERIORITY of OUR SYSTEM, in developing the *Natural Powers of Execution*,

And producing that ready and bold hand, so characteristic of

Business Writing.

We claim that every one may learn to write a good, easy, rapid business hand, and offer for

Twenty-five Dollars,

TO GUARANTEE

This result to any one, old or young.

This is not DECEPTION nor BRAGADOCIA, but a MATTER OF FACT, experienced by hundreds of seemingly hopeless cases,—young men, and old men,—who had practised other systems, at other Commercial Colleges and Schools, until they had come to the conviction that they were among the number, who could not

"Learn to Write,"

They had tried many times, spent much money, and were convinced

"'T WAS NO USE."

To such we say, COME, and we will show you the names and hand-writing of scores who like you, have become discouraged under the old system, and have declared

"OF WHAT USE IS IT LONGER TO TRY !"

TO MECHANICS.

ALMOST the first feature that strikes the eye of the stranger visiting our city, is the number of new and costly buildings constantly in process of erection. Though Providence is among the earliest settlements of New England, yet heretofore its public buildings nor private residences have taken rank as first-class architectural designs, but already the spirit of improvement is upon us, and capitalists are seeking first-class architects and mechanics, that the future city of Providence may be scientifically and intelligently built. How important is it, then, that the future builders of our city —the present apprentices,—should be scientifically instructed in the arts of designing, drafting and constructing. Messrs. George W. Cady and Edson S. Jones superintend the practical course of instruction in this department. The first-named gentleman gives his special attention to the subject of Geometrical Hand-Rail Drawing, and brings to the work an experience of twenty years of study and practice in this department of architecture.

Evening Instruction
— IS —
Mechanical Drafting,
Mechanical Calculations,

&c., will be given during the Fall and Winter, by competent and practical Teachers, among whom are Professors B. F. CLARK and ALEXANDER GRANT, besides other PRACTICAL GENTLEMEN from the various MACHINE SHOPS of the city.

The instruction is designed to be of the most PRACTICAL character, and calculated especially for *Pattern Makers, Machinists, Moulders, Carpenters, Tin and Sheet Iron Workers and Boiler Makers.*

Address W. W. WARNER.

THE story of the merchant who made the choice of a husband for his daughter depend on the one of two suitors who should write the best advertisement, serves to illustrate the importance business men attach to judicious advertising. There is only here and there one in any branch of business who looms up and fills the public eye and monopolizes the public purse. These are they who discriminate between the various mediums offered, and select only such as will be read, and preserved for their own intrinsic worth. That advertisers appreciate this fact, we have only to refer to the success of "OURS" ILLUSTRATED, published by Webb Bros. & Co., printed on new type, good paper, and containing "all the news." The illustrations are such designs as are calculated to cultivate a taste for the useful and the beautiful.

The first number of this valuable paper claims a date so far back only as last May, yet it has already reached a circulation of several thousand copies, and is expected to reach the round number of ten thousand in the October issue. Those who advertise in this paper and such as this, will be sure to obtain the full value of printer's ink. Let your advertisements have a sprinkling of "the dash" in them, and that, too, in your own language. If you cannot write it to suit you, come into the College, 164 Westminster street, and we will help you, and give you, in a few minutes, instruction which will be valuable through life.

Mason especially wanted to inspire women to come to the college. His 1865 circular stated that the Civil War had drawn men away from civilian life and opened up jobs for women. Before the war, the office had been strictly a male preserve, but, during the war, the United States government had taken the lead in employing women in offices. Mason saw this expansion of work opportunities as a positive step and commented, "It is now no unusual thing for posts of great importance and responsibility to be filled by women." He believed that this was the harbinger of even better things to come – "the establishment of 'woman's rights' in a true and noble sense." He assured the female readers that the Bryant and Stratton colleges had, from the beginning, offered the "advantages of a thorough commercial training" to women. He declared, "We have had the privilege of according Diplomas to young ladies whose thorough attainments in all the requisites of Accountantship would put to blush the pretensions of many a bearded competitor for like honors."[22] Female students remained a tiny minority for the next decade, but the college continued to advertise to attract women.

In 1866, Mason hired a man named Schuyler Grant to manage the college. Possibly he was feeling some of the frustrations other principals in the chain of colleges were expressing. In the 1860s, the principals had begun to meet in a yearly convention, and disagreements over management issues characterized their proceedings. By 1866, the rift among them was so serious that eight of them signed a letter to the effect that they had helped Bryant and Stratton become rich and famous and now deserved their independence.[23] In 1867, Stratton died and Henry Bryant decided to sell his own interests. The colleges were thus free to pay Stratton's heirs and Henry Bryant and dissolve the chain.

Mason, now independent, sold his college to William W. Warner and John J. Ladd. Ladd was soon out of the picture and Warner changed the college's name to Warner's Bryant and Stratton and then to Warner's Polytechnic Business College. He moved the college from place to place on Westminster Street and then settled it in the Hoppin Homestead Building in 1875. Warner felt expansive: courses in philosophy, history, Latin, Greek, Anglo-Saxon, Old German, Hebrew, modern German, French, Italian, and Spanish were advertised as available. (A Mr. Maximilian Berlitz was in charge of languages, briefly, then set up his own school in the same building and proceeded to build his empire of Berlitz schools.) In addition to these courses, Warner offered instruction in photography, sculpture, engineering, higher mathematics, hydraulics, steam engines, gears, cams, and screws.[24]

In 1872 Warner hired a young teacher, Theodore Stowell. This decision proved to be a turning point in the college's history. Stowell had distinguished himself for academic ability at Connecticut State Normal College at New Britain. One person described him as a "combination of Abraham Lincoln and keen businessman."[25] Within a few years, Stowell became principal and in 1878 he bought the college. For the next thirty-three years he remained in charge and developed Bryant and Stratton into a school specializing in business education, one respected in the state for the quality of its program and for the integrity of its leader.

Before Stowell took over, the faculty, which had once numbered eleven, had shrunk to three. He was determined to build up the faculty and the student body. (Warner's record-keeping may have been amiss or his records may have been lost; no documents remain to tell us how many students there were in 1878.) Stowell immediately ended the hodgepodge of courses Warner had dabbled in and returned the college to its original path of specialized education. He explained his objective:

Maximilian Berlitz taught foreign languages during Warner's tenure before founding his now famous Berlitz schools.

"In the domain of education it [Bryant and Stratton] stands for something as legitimate and distinct as do the professional courses in Brown University and in the public schools in the State."[26]

Stowell changed the name of the college back to "Bryant and Stratton Business School" and added "And Shorthand School." Later (1885), he added "And Typewriting School." He knew the importance of keeping up with the business needs of the time. Even as early as 1878, he realized that a revolution in office technology was occurring and that his college would have to offer instruction in operating these new machines. Indeed, changes in office practice necessitated changes in business education everywhere and affected Bryant and Stratton's student population and curriculum greatly in the last quarter of the century.

The technological revolution began in 1872 when an inventor, Christopher Sholes, patented a writing machine. He approached E. Remington and Sons, a firm which made guns and sewing machines, with the idea of manufacturing the machine. By the end of the decade, Remington was making and selling 1,500 typewriters a month and there were many competitors. By the 1880s the "typewriter"—meaning both the machine and the person who operated it—was fast becoming a standard office feature.[27]

Shorthand was not a new phenomenon like the typewriter: it had been a form of secret writing early in the nineteenth century and later was used to record speeches and sermons. However, the typewriter made shorthand viable in an office situation. Before the typewriter, a shorthand writer could take dictation, but the document then had to be written out by hand, a time-consuming procedure. With the advent of the typewriter, the document could be transcribed rapidly, and shorthand became a truly "short" method of business communication. Understandably, office managers sought people who were skilled in shorthand and typing.

In a very short time these tasks became "women's work." Probably the fact that they were both new tasks made it possible for offices to hire women to operate the typewriter and take dictation by the short method; a woman was not taking a man's job and was not upsetting office routine. Office managers could pay women less than men: men had a variety of better paying jobs available to them, whereas women had few alternatives.[28] They could work as domestic servants, saleswomen, seamstresses, or textile factory operatives but none of these paid as well as office work. In Rhode Island, in 1889, a saleswoman made $6.36 a week; seamstresses, $7.87; woolen mill workers, $5.38; but stenographers made $11.12.[29] Even college educated women went into office work since their alternatives were few, chiefly teaching or nursing. As a respectable occupation for women, requiring only a few months of training and paying well, office work won hands down.

Accordingly, the number of women in business schools increased: by 1914 they represented 57 percent of all students enrolled in office work courses.[30] Business schools had to reorganize their curriculum. Under Stowell's leadership, Bryant and Stratton in Providence was among the first to introduce shorthand. Beginning in the 1880s, the number of women students at Bryant and Stratton grew rapidly; although they continued to be a minority, they made up a sizeable group. Secretarial courses became an important part of the curriculum and continued to be so for almost a century.

There were other changes at Bryant and Stratton as well. Machines besides the typewriter had been invented in the late nineteenth century and students were seeking instruction in their use. The dictaphone, cash

Theodore Stowell taught for Warner before purchasing the college in 1878. Stowell narrowed the curriculum, reemphasizing business studies.

OPPOSITE:
The technological revolution in offices began with the invention of the "writing machine" in 1872. The typewriter created new jobs which were filled by women joining the workforce in the late 1800s.

register, accounting, calculating, adding, addressing, and mimeograph machines were all changing office practice and, consequently, business education. Stowell anticipated the growth of this technology and changed the curriculum at the college to include instruction in the new machines. An advertisement for Bryant and Stratton in the *Providence Board of Trade Journal* in 1908 informed the public: "Commercial education means more than a superficial knowledge of business forms; it requires a thorough training in Actual Business Practice and a familiarity with every mechanical labor-saving device used in the modern office."[31]

Stowell said he wanted to make business education like science education—completely taught in a laboratory. In 1884 he eliminated the preliminary period of formal instruction entirely and started the students immediately in practical work. He wrote, "A large number of young ladies and gentlemen were admitted last autumn and began to buy and sell goods and carry on real business as soon as they entered."[32] Students stayed approximately six months; later, in the twentieth century, Stowell extended the school term to ten months. Individuals learned by seeking instruction on how to deal with the problem at hand. One-to-one tutorials was the method of teaching. Even more than before, the school became a "community of business houses," including a retail store, the office of a manufacturing company, an extensive transportation company's office, a wholesale business, and a bank.[33] Students were expected to become proficient in bookkeeping, business arithmetic, business law, grammar, letter-writing, penmanship, and rhetoric and composition.

In 1897, the college counted 360 students and 11 teachers.

FACULTY

WALTER A. YOUNG, D.A. · HARVEY KINYON · THEODORE GOUTHIER · GRACE E. JAMES · WILLIAM H. SCOTT, A.M. · R. EMMA THOMPSON · EVERETT W. WHITFORD · ADIN S. HUBBARD · WM. B. SHERMAN · JEREMIAH C. BARBER

Attracting businessmen as teachers was important to the success of the college. They were experienced, pragmatic, and they hired graduates.

An advertisement in 1894 gives us a window on the scene. A visitor stood at the entrance of the main hall and described what he saw at Bryant and Stratton:

> "Is it recess?" the visitor asked, after gazing attentively for some minutes.
>
> "Recess!" said the amused principal. . . . "This is one of our workshops, and all these you see here are about their regular tasks. They are business men and women, attending with all their might to real mercantile transactions, carrying on trade and keeping their own accounts.
>
> "Just look at these books," he continued, taking up one and then another from the desks, and explaining with the eye of a practiced expert what each involved, and what knowledge of accounts the students must have in order to produce the work therein represented. It was plain that they were "learning by doing," as old Comenius counseled, but the work was all done under the eyes of careful inspectors who did not allow a single error to escape, and required the doer to understand the reason for everything he did.[34]

Because of the up-to-date curriculum and Stowell's leadership, the college grew. By 1897 there were eleven teachers and a student body of three hundred and sixty. The school had gained a fine reputation in the state: Bryant and Stratton graduates were recognized as having excellent penmanship and training. Brown University bestowed on Stowell the honorary degree of Master of Arts, attesting to the high regard the state's educators had for his work.[35]

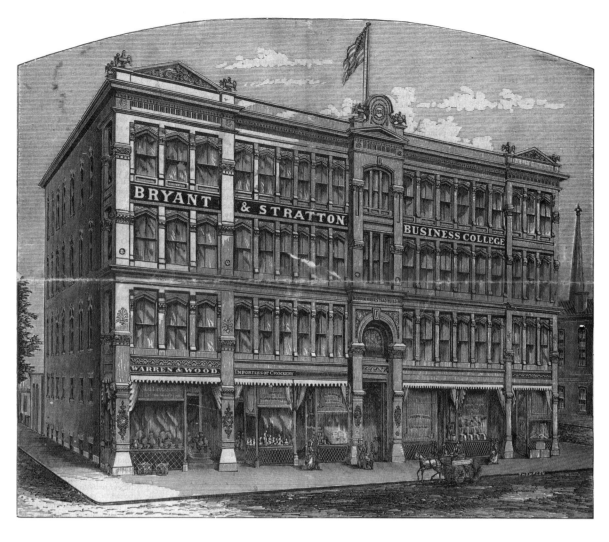

Continuity in staff and devotion to teaching characterized the school: William H. Scott taught office practice and banking at Bryant and Stratton from 1890 to 1927; William B. Sherman taught at Bryant and Stratton from 1890 to 1914; Jeremiah Barber, from 1897 to 1940.[36] Other teachers' names appear again and again in the catalogs over decades.

The college was fortunate in its location. The Hoppin Homestead building which housed Bryant and Stratton was constructed in 1876 and was considered very modern. The fourth floor was designed especially for the business college; under Stowell's leadership the college expanded and took up the third floor as well. Stowell's description made the place sound like a modern castle: there were 16,000 square feet of floor space, reached by a massive mahogany staircase or by an elevator from the ground floor. Walls were seventeen feet high. Every room was "well-lighted, ventilated, and heated by steam." The office where visitors were received was an "elegantly furnished room for private instruction." There was a "spacious" recitation room. The main hall, 38 feet by 66 feet, was furnished with solid black walnut counting-house tables and swivel-seat chairs. There were small recitation rooms. A hall, 28 feet by 54 feet, contained the simulated businesses for students' practice.[37]

The building was at 283 Westminster Street, an area bustling with commercial activity. In the late nineteenth century Westminster was lined with small businesses such as tailoring shops, office supply stores, insurance companies, tobacco shops, candle and church goods suppliers, booksellers such as Preston and Rounds Company, attorneys' offices, a

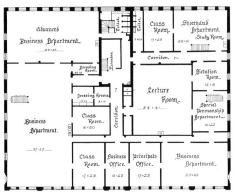

pharmacy, and a carriage and bicycle shop. The grand Hotel Dorrance stood on the corner of Westminster and Dorrance.[38] At the turn of the century Providence also boasted a number of theatres, assembly halls, and an opera house. Keith's Theatre on Westminster Street was a favorite.[39]

Rhode Island was the most densely populated state in the nation at the turn of the century. The percentage of immigrants in the population had grown since Bryant and Stratton had started their college. Now 65 percent of the population were men and women of foreign birth or foreign parentage. Most worked in manufacturing plants–less than one-sixth still farmed.[40] Wages were low, hours long, and accounts of strikes filled the newspapers. Three great trust companies dominated Rhode Island's financial affairs: The Industrial, The Union, and the Rhode Island Hospital Trusts. Woolen and cotton manufactures were in the hands of a few men. Although horse owners complained about the "high-wheeled menace," rubber for bicycle tires was a profitable business.[41] Davol Rubber Company, organized in 1875 under the name of Perkins Manufacturing Company, made rubber, as did the Mechanical Fabric Company.

Not only was the city humming with industry, it had also become the capital of the state. In spite of recurring financial recessions and labor unrest, Providence continued to be a good location for a business school with numbers of offices opening up, both commercial and government.

In the last few years before World War I, Bryant and Stratton faced plenty of competition: five commercial schools were now located in downtown Providence. The first, Scholfield's, had been going since 1846; Bryant and Stratton was the second. In 1911, a widow, Katherine Gibbs, sold her jewelry and rented a building in downtown Providence to establish a school to teach women how to take shorthand and type. In 1914 Gertrude Johnson and Mary Wales started a school devoted to

*Providence's early factories
employed a large number of
immigrant workers. Wages were
low. At the Davol Rubber
Company, rubber was made for
the tires of the "high-wheeled
menace"–the bicycle.*

The Butler Exchange Building (the imposing structure on the right) was located in the city's transportation hub. It was the home of the Rhode Island Commercial School, one of Bryant and Stratton's chief competitors.

business education for women. In addition, there was the Rhode Island Commercial School, founded in 1898, and since 1907 owned and operated by Harry Loeb Jacobs in the Butler Exchange Building.

Jacobs, Stowell's chief competitor, had grown up in Dayton, Ohio. He had been educated in private schools and had spent a year studying law at the University of Michigan. As a very young man, he had learned how to take shorthand and had become secretary to a senator, travelling around the country with him.[42] Later, he had served as official reporter for the Pennsylvania legislature, and had opened a business school in Dayton (now known as Miami-Jacobs College). He had then sold his business school to buy a chain of dime stores in New York State. Realizing that a small operation like his could not compete with huge, nationwide chains, he had sold his dime stores and had come to assist the ailing head of the Rhode Island Commercial School, Adelbert Heaney.

Harry Jacobs owned the Rhode Island Commercial School and was ready to expand just as Stowell was preparing to retire. Jacobs bought Bryant and Stratton and merged the two schools.

Jacobs was assistant principal for one year and the next year, 1907, he bought the school.[43] A student at the Rhode Island Commercial School in 1908, Ethel Barmingham, remembered Harry Jacobs as an impressive figure – handsome, neatly dressed, courteous, and commanding respect. When he was in the building, everybody sat up straight, she said.[44]

Jacobs proceeded to improve the school's public relations – a task for which he had a special talent. He regularly published a paper, *Business Training,* which told the public what was happening at Rhode Island Commercial School. He planned graduations so that he could win publicity, compel the most notable citizens to come to the school, and fill the graduates with lifelong loyalty. The list of graduates always appeared in the local newspapers. At the August 1914 graduation, the mayor of Providence, Joseph Gainer, a congressman, and several leading members of the clergy spoke. The mayor remarked, "Last year was the first time I attended these exercises, and I was surprised to learn that Mr. Jacobs had so large a school." He added, "I believe that many people in the city of Providence do not yet realize what a large school the Rhode Island Commercial School is." He expressed the appreciation of the city of Providence for what Jacobs had done "to raise the standard of commercial education."[45] Tangible proof of Jacobs' success could be seen in the growth of the school. When he purchased it, there had been only 70 students. By 1914, the graduating class had 150.[46]

By 1916, the Rhode Island Commercial School was doing so well that Jacobs was ready to expand. He offered to buy Bryant and Stratton. The aging Theodore Stowell was impressed with Jacobs and agreed to sell. Jacobs moved Bryant and Stratton to the Butler Exchange Building and merged it with the Rhode Island Commercial School. A charter of incorporation was issued in the office of the Secretary of State for Rhode Island to Bryant and Stratton Rhode Island Commercial School stating that the value of the capital stock was $100,000.[47] The incorporators were listed as Harry L. Jacobs, T. B. Stowell, Thomas Zanslauer Lee, Hattie E. Jacobs (Mrs. Harry L. Jacobs), and Rothsay T. Clemens. Stowell told a newspaper reporter that the merger enabled him to "transfer the work of the executive management to the shoulder of a younger man."[48] Stowell became president emeritus but he lived only a month after the sale of his school.

Always with an eye to the competition, Jacobs saw that enrollment gains were occurring in many colleges and universities which had begun to offer majors in business just before World War I.[49] He realized that to meet this new competition his college would have to take another major step. His efforts at publicizing the value of commercial education and at making people in the state aware of the college now had important results: in 1916 he persuaded the state legislature to empower his college to grant degrees.[50] Now Bryant and Stratton Rhode Island Commercial College could give its students a Bachelor of Commercial Science or a Bachelor of Accounts. This was a feat his competitors in the city could not match; nevertheless, by granting degrees at Bryant, he enhanced the prestige of a business education in general as well as the prestige of his institution. Bryant and Stratton was now in fact a college: from this point on it changed to meet the expectations and requirements of its new status.

To qualify for degree-granting privileges, there was a reorganization. Jacobs hired consultants from the New York University business department and from the Harvard Graduate School of Business. He said, "The idea was to lay out an honest, sound kind of education in business on a higher level than a commercial school."[51] Now students could no longer enter the school whenever they wished, and requirements for admission were defined. Only people with a high school diploma could enter the degree program. Learning took place in formal classes rather than in a mock store or a mock bank and the length of time to complete a degree was set at two years, each term lasting eleven months.

The new courses were delineated: a student could take the Business Administration Course (a two-year program with emphasis on accounting and business administration), the Shorthand Course (a brief pro-

gram), or the Secretarial Course (two years with courses in accounting and business administration as well as courses in English, shorthand, and typing). The two-year programs led to the bachelor's degree; the Shorthand Course, to a diploma.

Jacobs continuously upgraded the curriculum by introducing more advanced courses than business schools usually offered. Bryant and Stratton had offered bookkeeping and auditing before he took over, but he had his eye on developments in that field and knew changes would have to be made. In 1906 a chapter of Certified Public Accountants had been organized in Rhode Island, and by 1917, accountants had to pass a stiff examination to qualify for this profession. Jacobs hired Warren Lane, CPA, to come to the college and head the program in accounting. In 1918 Bryant and Stratton began offering the Pace and Pace course in accounting, acknowledged even then as providing the best texts and methods in the nation.[52]

When public high schools began to teach commercial subjects, a scarcity of well-trained commercial teachers was the result. The college responded by offering the two-year Commercial Teacher's Training Course culminating in a degree for those who wanted to teach.

The college also offered non-degree courses designed to help adult students. For example, people had to pass civil service examinations for such positions as railway mail clerk, post office service clerk, and rural delivery clerk. The college offered a curriculum in preparation for these tests. Besides the usual courses in arithmetic, report writing, bookkeeping, penmanship, shorthand and typing, this curriculum included "Geography and Civil Government of the United States." There was also a preparatory course, described as a "Review of Common School Studies," for those students who, "through force of circumstances," had left school at an early age and therefore had not acquired the necessary fundamental knowledge to take up advanced work.[53] In this way, bright and hard-working adults could prepare themselves to enter a degree-granting program.

Other colleges in the state were also developing in the first decades of the new century. Providence College was chartered in 1917 and opened in 1919. The Rhode Island School of Design, begun in 1877, was growing and defining its curriculum. The Rhode Island Normal School, chartered in 1871 to prepare teachers for the state's schools, took a new name, The Rhode Island College of Education, in 1920. The state had begun an agricultural experiment station and school for the agricultural and mechanical arts at Kingston in 1888 and designated this as the Rhode Island State College in 1909.

In 1916, as Bryant and Stratton became a degree-granting institution, it also defined its curriculum, teaching methods, and calendar—establishing the structure it would retain for the first half of the twentieth century. Harry Loeb Jacobs, an astute businessman, was firmly in charge and was destined to be the president for the next forty-five years.

The merged Bryant and Stratton Rhode Island Commercial School was located in the Butler Exchange Building from 1916 to 1925.

The 1920s and 1930s: Lean Years and Good Times

ARRY LOEB JACOBS' purchase of Bryant and Stratton in 1916 reveals a good eye for a business opportunity as well as a fine sense of timing. He quickly devised three strategies. He would open the college a little earlier in the fall than his competitors so that students would have to make an early decision and would be more likely to choose Bryant. He would invest the fall tuition wisely, dispersing the sum over the year so that part of the money was always working for the college. Also, there would be no unnecessary expenses – it would be a "no frills" situation.

Jacobs predicted that the post-World War I era would bring in a flood of veterans. He was right: in the 1918–19 school year, 1,965 students registered at the Providence Bryant and Stratton Commercial School.[1] This sudden swelling of enrollment was typical of what was happening throughout the country.[2] Bryant and Stratton was already a profitable concern and the influx of veterans gave it an even greater boost financially than it had enjoyed after the Civil War. However, the postwar increase in the number of students ceased at Bryant and Stratton in the early twenties as it did in the nation at large.[3] Bryant's enrollment leveled off at about 1,200. Of course, many took only a few courses and did not work towards a degree or diploma. At graduation there would usually be about 250 students.

As the college prospered in the early 1920s, Jacobs looked for better facilities for Bryant and Stratton. In the spring of 1925, the college was moved to the brand new eight-story, fireproof Gardner Building. Teachers, students, and moving men worked together. The new building at 40 Fountain Street was in the midst of action: just around the corner, Fay's Theatre showed vaudeville, the Arcadia Dance hall spewed music a block away, and a burlesque house farther down the street advertised its charms. Electric streetcars brought Bryant and Stratton students close to the college's doors.[4]

Upstairs, on the sixth, seventh, and eighth floors, 30,000 square feet of space housed Bryant and Stratton. Jacobs planned the details so that the environment would be conducive to learning. He was especially concerned with lighting design so that studying and writing would be facilitated by good light. The lighting system was the latest in technology and came from Westinghouse Lighting Laboratories of New York.[5] The offices had a soft tan tint on the walls, sand-colored draperies, two-toned

Jacobs enhanced the college's public image by inviting nationally prominent people to receive honorary degrees. Vice President Charles Curtis (above left) came to Providence to be honored in 1930. Henry Ford (below) accepted a degree, but did not appear in person at the graduation ceremony.

In 1925 the college moved to larger quarters in the Gardner Building on Washington Street. Constructed in 1918 for the R. L. Greene Paper Co., the building got its name from company president Nathan L. Gardner. The college purchased and enlarged the building, adding the top two floors for school use.

brown rugs, and mahogany furniture. In addition to classrooms and offices, a reference library and conference rooms, there was an assembly hall. Ceilings were fourteen feet high; windows were abundant; and there was an ambiance of spaciousness and elegance. It was modern, as well: the facilities included a lunch counter described as "electrically equipped."[6]

Jacobs was jubilant over this urban campus. On the evening of March 11, 1925, the faculty and students were hosts to several hundred guests at a housewarming. Flowers were everywhere, refreshments were in abundance, and music was in the air. At nine o'clock, the speeches began. Harry Jacobs welcomed everyone, and alumni such as Senator Sidney Clifford praised Jacobs as a worthy successor to the school's founders. On the way out, guests picked up souvenir calendars.[7]

Conscious of the importance of public relations to continued success, Jacobs appointed an advisory board which included the governor of Rhode Island, the mayor of Providence, the president of the Chamber of Commerce, a bank director, and several heads of local manufacturing companies. He also endeavored to bring nationally known people to the college. He would meet them socially at resorts in Florida, correspond for a year, then invite them to come to Bryant and Stratton to receive an honorary degree. John Robert Gregg, inventor of the shorthand method that had come into general use, was one of the notables who travelled to Bryant and Stratton to be honored.[8] One year, Vice President of the United States Charles Curtis, United States Senator Jesse H. Metcalf, and State Finance Commissioner Fred S. Peck attended the college's graduation ceremonies to receive honorary degrees.[9]

Jacobs invited Henry Ford to receive a doctorate. Ford always refused such honors and so declined the invitation. Jacobs persisted, describing Bryant's concentration on preparing students in an accelerated business program. Ford relented: "You say you turn 'em out in two years—why, that's the way I make Fords." He did not attend graduation, but he said he would accept an honorary master's. A stand-in picked up the degree for him at the 1931 graduation.[10]

This talent for good public relations was also expressed in publications. Jacobs regularly published not only a college catalog but also a periodical, *Earning Power*, which featured articles describing events at the college as well as individual success stories. Of course, these stories stressed the value of business education. One article on accounting had the following headlines: "The Highest Paid Profession—Salaries of from $5,000.00 to $25,000.00 a Year Not Uncommon Among Its Members."[11] Readers were assured that accounting was not difficult with the step-by-step methods used by the "practical instructors" at Bryant and Stratton. In reality, the promise was not hollow. Many working-class young men and women came to Bryant and Stratton through financial sacrifice on the part of their parents. They worked at part-time jobs, studied hard, and achieved success in a business career.

In one biography of a woman who started out as a general office girl and ended up owning her own insurance company, the reader of *Earning Power* was reminded: "But in business school she had learned that every position has its opportunities if they are developed."[12] Another story advised, "Whether You Are Planning for a Home or a Career, This article

Will Help You." It began, "Every woman should spend at least two or three years in a business office before she assumes the responsibilities of marriage." The writer went on to say that the business world offered the young woman a chance to become independent. She didn't have to marry for the sake of "landing a breadwinner." The young woman who graduated from a business college would find a career so attractive that she might "advance up the ladder to a high-salaried position." And a cheerful note held out this golden promise: "Many young women, both wives and mothers, are finding time to manage both their homes and businesses."[13] Unfortunately, the statistics suggest that very few women who trained for office work ever progressed to become managers; society was not ready for women bosses. Nevertheless, there is no doubt that many women found that their education at Bryant and Stratton was a means of achieving economic independence.

Like every good businessman, Jacobs was aware that to be successful he had to turn out an excellent product. He made sure that he put people in charge who were absolutely devoted to the rigorous training of

students. One such person was his vice president, Percy Jamison, a big, full-bodied man with an outgoing personality and a serious interest in teaching. Jacobs would spot an excellent student—someone with intelligence, drive, and integrity—and offer the man or woman a job at Bryant. Several outstanding students, graduates in the twenties and thirties, joined the staff and served the college for decades.

Nelson Gulski was such a student: he graduated in 1925 and immediately began teaching accounting. He later became dean of the Division of Business

Administration, then vice president, and in 1969 and 1975 acting president. George Craig graduated in 1929, went to work for Bryant as bursar, later joined the admissions office, and in 1967 became director of admissions and served in that post until his retirement in 1975. John Allan, an early graduate (1918) of Bryant's accounting program, was hired as bursar, worked his way up to become the chief financial officer, and served as Harry Jacobs' "right-hand man" in the thirties, forties, and early fifties. He became vice president just a year before his untimely death in 1956. Lionel Mercier, also an early Bryant graduate (1930), returned to teach in 1939, became dean of the School of Business Teacher Education and Secretarial Science, and later, assistant to the president and vice president for academic affairs. He retired in the early seventies. Lucien Appleby (always called Ray) graduated in 1927, worked in the college's financial office, became vice president and treasurer, and served the college until his death in 1968.

Jacobs insisted on excellent work in the classroom. In the mid-twenties, when Nelson Gulski entered the accounting program at Bryant and Stratton, he found that classes were taught on a lecture and problem-solving basis. Warren Lane, who taught most of the accounting courses, was tall and somewhat stooped, with a close-clipped black mustache. He had a Southern drawl and a dry sense of humor. He would tell his students enough–but never too much. He liked to get his students into an argument about an accounting problem, then happily walk off to let them debate and research for themselves.

Although course work was very demanding during the 1920s there was still plenty of time for extracurricular activities, including athletics and student publications.

The accounting program was so highly demanding that of the thirty students who started with Gulski, only sixteen finished.[14] While the accounting course had the reputation of being the most formidable, both the general business course and the stenographic course had high standards as well. The rapid pace kept the students working fall, winter, spring, and summer for two years with only a Christmas holiday and two weeks of vacation in August.

However, students at the college in the mid-twenties had a good time–it wasn't all work. There was always a Christmas party with a huge tree and an appearance by Santa Claus. Each department had a dance, and the evening school had a vaudeville program on Awards Night at the end of May. The student actors in the dramatic society produced plays and a college orchestra entertained at special events. A basketball team played other teams in the city.

At the end of their college experience, Bryant and Stratton students could look forward to help in finding a job. Jacobs hired Ida Knight to be the full-time director of student welfare and placement.[15] The tradition of cultivating contacts with businessmen with the aim of placing graduates in jobs continued. Jacobs met the local business leaders in civic groups and entertained them at the college and in his home.

In the mid-twenties, Bryant and Stratton was over half a century old. Testimonials from graduates abounded in the college publications. A typical testimonial came from F. M. Mason at the Providence Institute of Savings:

> As my mind goes back over the forty years that have passed since I attended Bryant and Stratton College, I am impressed with the solid foundation that you lay for a business life.
>
> During those forty years I have been associated continually with students that have graduated from the college at later periods, my own son being one, and I find that the thorough training of the earlier years has been continued to the present time.[16]

The college made its graduates an important part of recruiting and public relations efforts. These prominent Rhode Island alumni were members of the advisory board and were featured in college catalogues.

However, the optimism about employment and success vanished with the financial crash at the end of the decade. Beginning in 1929 the college experienced the Depression's effects: it was harder to find jobs for graduates, and the college enrollment dropped. The number of students graduating fell from 240 in 1929 to 171 in 1930.[17]

Jacobs' wise management enabled Bryant and Stratton to survive when many small colleges were failing. He said,

> The early years were a constant financial sacrifice on the part of myself and my family. However, obligations were met, bills paid, and hundreds of men and women prepared for a satisfactory livelihood in the world of business.[18]

Jacobs always tried to have investments that the school could fall back on in a crisis. During the Depression he not only had to sell some of the investments, but he was forced to dig into his own pocket and the pockets of his faculty. After the crash of 1929, he met the faculty several times and described to them the general financial picture. They were not used to being consulted and remained silent. One day, he told them point-blank that their salaries would be cut by ten percent. "Prices have dropped—you can get by," he said.[19]

Slowly the number of students rose again and by 1935 and 1936 the college was graduating 250 students once more. Although the early thirties were lean years, the people in charge were most able. In the late twenties and early thirties, Jeremiah C. Barber (known around the school as J. C.) was head of the business administration department. He had been a teacher when Jacobs bought the school and by the thirties he could be recognized instantly by his snow-white hair and mustache, and huge frame. He tolerated no foolishness from anyone, but students soon became aware of his sensitivity to their feelings and concern for them. Elmer Wilbur headed the secretarial department. He was clean-shaven, had a reddish tinge to his hair, a ready smile, a quick answer, and sometimes a sharp tongue. The tall and handsome former student John Allan, now executive secretary, made sure the budget was adhered to.[20]

In the thirties, these three, Allan, Wilbur, and Barber, managed the school on a day-to-day basis. But there was no doubt that everyone—from the janitor up to the executive secretary—took orders from Harry Jacobs. He was an assiduous supervisor, checking on the smallest detail to make sure the college was well-managed. People remembered a gesture symbolic of this: he would run his white-gloved fingers along the ledges of the wall to see if anyone had left a speck of dust.[21]

In 1930 Jacobs' wife, Harriet Einstein Jacobs, died, and this loss, plus worries over the country's economic depression and the college's survival, took their toll. His sometimes severe facial expressions were anxiously watched.[22]

Jacobs' son, Gardner Jacobs, now in his late twenties, had received his degree at Bryant and Stratton. He had done all kinds of work at the college—everything except sweeping the sidewalks, he said.[23] In the 1920s and 1930s, he went around the city, arranging for private homes to

Bryant and Stratton's Monthly Letter on Current Business Conditions predicted that the country was headed for a recession in July 1929.

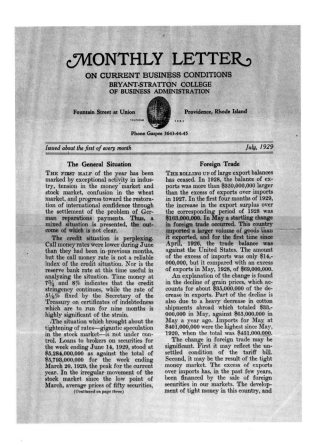

Fraternities competed for the interfraternal bowling trophy in the early 1930s.

take in students who came from outside the state and needed places to live. He was often on the road, speaking at high schools, trying to interest students in coming to Bryant and Stratton. When he was at the college, he coached athletic activities and worked on job placement.[24] Gardner Jacobs became vice president in the early thirties, but his father made it clear that it was Harry Jacobs who was the real boss.

A student newspaper, the *Bryant-Stratton News*, was begun in the thirties, with a cost per issue of five cents. Sororities and fraternities had sprung up early in the decade. These organizations now sponsored social events and also encouraged intramural sports. All these activities received dramatic coverage in the *Bryant-Stratton News*. The announcement of Stunt Night, an annual affair begun in 1932, gives an idea of the flavor of its reporting. According to the paper, it was to be a "night when gloom and dull care are cast aside and all the college blazes forth in a galaxy of stars, comedians, and ham actors." The promise was made: "We shall see art that is art. We shall see acting that is acting, and isn't." On the same day, the seniors were visiting the International Business Machines showrooms on Broad Street to look at the new Hollerith Accounting Machine—"a very intricate and ingenious device." And the varsity basketball team—the Indians—was training for the alumni game. The paper's writers hinted at romances and made droll comments on student life. One aspect of social life was suggested: "Several of the freshmen could get to the Puritan or Blue Moon (bars) blind-folded—they know the road so well, having been there so often lately."[25] Theatres in downtown Providence had now become movie houses, and advertisements of the latest films beckoned students there.

However, the tough year-round schedule kept students busy with academic work most of the time. There was a new note in the educational rhetoric in the 1930s: the catalogue described "A Liberal Business Education" at Bryant and Stratton. Business required a broader training than was thought sufficient in the past, the catalogue informed the reader. Now, clear thinking, sound judgment, cultural sophistication, and good character were required by young men and women seeking preferred positions in business. The technical courses were still there: accountancy, finance, transportation, marketing, organization, management, and secretarial studies. But now students could also choose to take psychology, English, economics, public speaking, and personality development.[26] The catalogue declared: "It is a college education as thorough and scholarly as that afforded by the older type classical college in its field, but the curriculum is especially planned to satisfy the practical and exacting demands of business." The motto was still, "From campus to career in two years," and this continued to have strong appeal to the career-minded.[27]

Bryant and Stratton had been training people to teach commercial subjects in high school since Harry Jacobs reorganized the curriculum in the first few years after he bought the college. In 1927, Bryant and

Stratton and the Rhode Island College of Education cooperated in training students to teach commercial subjects: the student went two years to Rhode Island College, then two years to Bryant. But in 1937, students began to take all their courses at Bryant during a four-and-a-half-year program which included a semester of practice teaching. They received the degree of Bachelor of Secretarial Science in Commercial Education. At the time this was the only commercial teacher's course in Rhode Island approved by the Rhode Island Board of Education.[28]

Both Rhode Island Commercial School and Bryant and Stratton were holding evening classes in 1916, and after the merger, the evening program continued in full swing, offering courses of special interest to adults in the community throughout the twenties. The Evening Division was further expanded in the 1930s. Courses were organized in two separate programs: one offered advanced courses in business administration, accountancy, finance, and administrative-secretarial training. These led to the Bachelor of Science degree. The other program contained introductory courses in secretarial practice, basic accounting, and other subjects needed to qualify for entry into the degree program. Whether day or evening, Bryant and Stratton accepted only high school graduates into the degree program; but often adult students who already had a high school diploma took courses in preparation for admission. Others who wanted certain courses in sequence could work towards a certificate.

All students, day and evening, began in September. Sessions for the degree courses in the Evening Division met Monday, Wednesday, and Friday evenings from 7:00 to 9:15. The preparatory courses met Tuesday and Thursday evenings for two and a half hours. The same faculty taught both the evening degree courses and the day courses. They accepted the fact that part of their teaching assignment would be in the Evening Division, and it was a heavy teaching load by today's standards—twenty hours a week during the day and two evenings of two and a half hours each. The full year's tuition in the Evening Division was $110, payable in four installments. Thus, in the thirties, a working man or woman could earn a college degree going to Bryant at night for four years at a total cost of $440. (However, the degree read "Evening Division"—the custom everywhere—although faculty and courses were the same as in the day.)

In the mid-thirties, students were coming to the college in increasing numbers. There were now students from thirty-six states and several foreign countries. Lack of classroom space became a problem and faculty worried that they would not be able to give students individual attention when it was needed. In 1937 the decision was made to limit enrollment of day students to 500.[29]

Even with limitations on enrollment, the facilities did not offer enough space. The basketball team played in the city high school's gymnasium. Graduation ceremonies were held in rented quarters—the Albee Theatre. Dances and parties had to go on in rented halls. The downtown area was noisy and crowded, and there was no possibility of the college expanding there.

Harry Jacobs had had his eye on Providence's East Side as a future site for the college. In the early twenties, he had purchased a lot on College Hill (the present site of the Rhode Island School of Design refectory). Irate Brown University students yanked up the sign—"Future Home of Bryant College"—and threw it in the river.[30]

In 1935 a large structure came up for long-term lease at the corner of Young Orchard Avenue and Hope Street, and Harry Jacobs jumped at the

This catchy phrase was used throughout the 1920s and 1930s on Evening Division catalogues. At night, students could complete degrees or improve their job skills.

In 1935, Jacobs purchased the Hope Hospital and its grounds on the corner of Hope Street and Young Orchard Avenue on the city's East Side. This new and rather splendid college building was renamed South Hall.

chance to lease it and move the college to the East Side. The elegant building had a long history: in the nineteenth century, it had been the home of Rhode Island's famous manufacturing family, the Spragues. Isaac Gifford Ladd, a broker, had purchased the three-story brick mansion at the turn of the century and spent a million dollars remodeling it.[31] He had made it look like a French chateau. Most recently it had been the Hope Hospital.

Harry Jacobs spent $5,000 to convert the hospital into a college.[32] A new building was constructed between what had been the carriage house and the nurses' quarters. It provided a basketball court, stage, dressing rooms, and back stage space as well as a gym, assembly hall, and eating areas for the cafeteria in the attached building. Students fondly referred to it as the "cafegymnatorium."

Harry Jacobs decided the college should have a new identity. The name "Bryant and Stratton" had earlier carried some prestige; now it was linked to the image of an old-time business school. With its upgraded courses and degree-granting programs, the college was a far different place now. After considerable discussion of possible names (including North-eastern College of Commerce), the new name was chosen – Bryant College of Business Administration.[33] The new Bryant College moved to the East Side on August 1, 1935, and all was ready for students by September 3.

As the college changed its location, it also changed its name to Bryant College of Business Administration.

Faculty and students were thrilled. There were two and a half acres of land with *grass*; the college now had a real campus. Now, in Class Day exercises, graduates marched through the archway at South Hall – a splendid symbol which would become a tradition. And there was an unexpected bonus: as Nelson Gulski remarked, "Holding forth in the old operating room with its lingering odor of ether reminded one of the seriousness of life."[34]

Gradually, the college expanded as homes in the neighborhood came up for sale. In 1939 Harry Jacobs bought a twelve-room Victorian house at 14 Young Orchard Avenue to use as classroom space.[35] Most students were commuters, riding streetcars or boarding trains from South County or Burrillville, but the college was attracting more and more out-of-state students. At first, women from other states lived at St. Maria's Home, the YWCA, or in a house called "Bryant Hall." Gardner Jacobs was determined to provide housing for students within walking distance of the college. In 1938 he bought two houses and remodeled them for use as dormitories.[36] The next year, he bought another house and took long-term leases on two more.[37] The year after that, he bought a large residence at 131 Hope Street.[38] He kept watching for private homes which he could purchase or lease and use as residence halls. Brown University kept its watch as well, and often the university and Bryant coveted the same property. The two were cousins in the education family—but not kissing cousins. Mutual tolerance characterized their relationship in this elegant but crowded area of the city.

In terms of having a campus and possibilities for expansion, the college was in its best location yet. If Bryant and Stratton had remained in the city's business center, it could not have developed into a residential college. And the change in name, as well as the addition of liberal arts courses to the curriculum, signified a resolution on the part of Jacobs and the faculty and administration to continue to develop the institution along the lines of a traditional college.

The thirties were financially difficult years for higher education in general. Nelson Gulski remarked that it took courage and foresight to undertake a major investment and move in the mid-thirties. But when other leaders in small colleges wondered if there would be a future, Jacobs was certain of Bryant's.

On the East Side, the college was able to expand and provide more student housing. Bryant Hall (above) on Hope Street was the first women's dormitory.

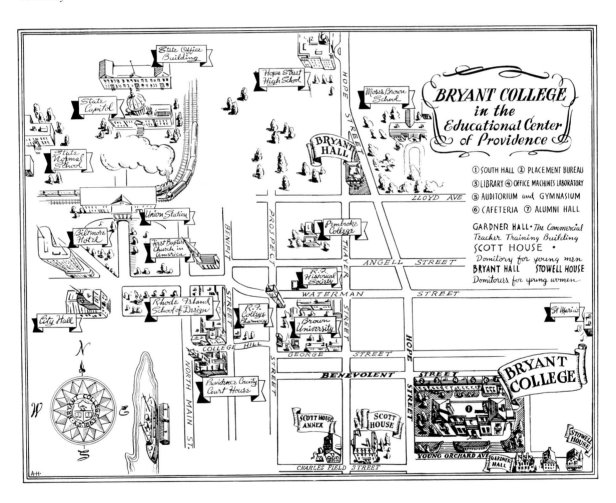

OVERLEAF:
South Hall provided a stately campus center. Behind it a new building was added which included a cafeteria, stage, gymnasium and assembly hall.

East Siders: Bryant College in the 1940s and 1950s

WORLD WAR II changed the college in ways no one had anticipated. At first, enrollment began dropping and fell to a near-disaster point: there were 250 graduates in 1942, 205 graduates in 1943; but only 10 men and 143 women graduated in 1944.[1] Harry Jacobs quoted the old saying, "When you think you're at the end of your rope, tie a knot and hang on."[2]

In 1942 a supplement to the college catalogue – "Special War Emergency Programs of Bryant College" – described courses to prepare people to step into civilian jobs left by the drafted men and also new jobs in industry and government arising from war needs. Particularly there was a shortage of well-trained office workers, and the college offered several twenty-four week intensive programs in this field. For example, there was a program for college graduates which included shorthand, typing, and office machines. Later, a pamphlet, "Calling All G.I.s," informed veterans of educational opportunities for them.[3]

Gardner Jacobs surmised that men who had been out of school four or five years and had been fighting a war might have some doubts about their ability to be students again. Although the G.I. Bill made college financially possible, many had never dreamed of going to college and had not prepared themselves in high school for college entrance. He devised a "refresher program" which provided an intensive review of arithmetic, English, and bookkeeping.[4] In some cases, veterans came to Bryant to take this course in preparation for the examination for a high school diploma. They could enter the "refresher program" at any time they wished. Admissions counselors placed pamphlets in veterans' centers informing veterans about this program and other advantages at Bryant.

After 1945, enrollment started increasing. Many veterans felt that, as older students, they had no time to waste; a two-year program was appealing. Many liked the idea of a refresher course as a starting point. In 1946, 1947, and 1948 the number of students reached 2,100 a year in facilities that normally served about 1,000 students. Enrollment peaked in 1949 at 3,000 students.[5] The college tried to hire additional staff, but that was not easy because there was a desperate need for faculty in colleges all over the nation. Nelson Gulski, who had become head of the

Bryant experienced an influx of students after World War II. Refresher programs were designed to meet the veterans' needs.

Business Administration and Accounting Division, said that the college was lucky if it had one applicant for each opening.[6]

Gulski and Lionel Mercier, who headed the teacher education and secretarial programs, began in 1945 to figure out how to cope with this increase in the number of students. They invented a "warm seat system." Said Gulski, "We'd bring one group in at half past seven in the morning and run them four classes in a row, send them to lunch and bring in another class for one period, send them to lunch, bring the first group back for an hour and then send them home and bring the second group back in again—we'd end up about four o'clock."[7] Evening classes began at seven o'clock.

Instructors enjoyed teaching the veterans and felt the older students brought business experience and maturity to the classroom. Many veterans had started families. They were eager to do well in college, and they were serious students, but they also had to work at part-time jobs. They had no time to participate in extracurricular activities. Their fellow students regarded them with awe. Herbert McLaughlin, who was a nineteen-year-old student at Bryant in 1949 (and later, a professor of law) remarked, "I was still a kid... they were a lot more mature than I was."[8] But in spite of differences in age and experience, young students and veterans occasionally formed friendships and helping relationships.

The Veterans Administration paid for tuition and fees, even books and supplies, but not for room and board. Married veterans found their own houses; however, the college made appeals to the public to provide good housing for veterans, married and single.

Single men sometimes made their own arrangements in the second year at Bryant. Dominic Falcone, who came to Bryant in 1948 after four years in the navy, described a typical situation. When he was a freshman, he lived in a college-approved boarding house at 429 Angell Street. The next year, he rented an apartment with four other students. Each person contributed $5.00 a week for groceries. They shared household tasks—Dominic did the food shopping and cooking.[9]

All out-of-town single women students, unless they were over twenty-one, were required to live in college-supervised residences. The college was in desperate need of space, so Gardner Jacobs and George Craig walked the blocks around the East Side, looking for houses to lease. When they found a place, they had to find housemothers, cooks, and cleaning personnel to staff the residence. Sometimes they were able to persuade sedate East Side widows to open their homes to students and serve as housemothers.

The "warm

As enrollment increased so did the need for space. A beautiful house across Hope Street from South Hall became the administration building in 1947.

Formal balls were a favorite college tradition. Rhodes on the Pawtuxet was the site of this 1949 dance.

seat" triple sessions brought in unprecedented income,[10] and most of this was plowed back into buying homes for classrooms or dormitories and into renovating these facilities. In 1947 the college bought a stylish fourteen-room brick Georgian house at 154 Hope Street (at the corner of Hope and Benevolent Streets) for use as an administration building.[11] (From then on, faculty referred to administrators as "the folks across the street.") This cleared additional space for classrooms in South Hall. The next year, Harry Jacobs purchased a lot bounded by Butler Avenue, Pitman and East George Streets to be used as a field for intramural athletics.[12] The college leased an additional nine homes for dormitories. At the end of 1949, there were thirteen buildings in all–classroom buildings, the administration building, and dormitories–spread over three blocks.[13] All in all, the sum of $250,000 was used to expand and enlarge the college in 1947–49.[14] And yet, there was still not enough room. The library was too small, and professors' offices were often closets adjoining a classroom or tiny rooms with several professors sharing.

Harry Jacobs regularly took a long winter vacation. He would call from West Palm Beach and spend several hours talking to his chief administrators. On one such leave, Gardner Jacobs proceeded to build an addition to the campus, a structure which he decided to call Memorial Hall. When Harry Jacobs returned in early spring and saw the steam shovels preparing the site, he was irate. He realized that a major decision had been made without him. Gardner Jacobs reflected on their relationship, "He controlled everyone but me–we had some kind of arguments! But just the same, things worked out all right."[15] Work on Memorial Hall continued.

Harry Jacobs was in his mid-seventies in 1948 and was worrying about what would happen to the college after his death. He now saw Bryant as an institution which transcended his personal interests or the interests of his family. In April 1948, he shocked the educational world by offering Bryant College to Brown University as an outright gift. He was able to get a bill introduced in the Rhode Island legislature which made Bryant a tax-exempt, non-profit institution which eventually would become the property of Brown University. He explained the decision to a reporter from the *Providence Journal*: ". . . it has become an institution. . . when I pass out of the picture, I'd hate to see it fall to people who might make a mess of it, or destroy its values."[16] Henry M. Wriston, Brown's president, described the offer as "generous," but he was puzzled by this unprecedented act. He remarked, "I don't think such a thing has happened before, and it is a very unusual idea."[17]

At this time, the student body at Bryant numbered 3,000 and the property was valued at one million dollars. The offer was made on condition that Brown operate a "Bryant College of Business Administration" as an integral part of the university.[18] Jacobs may well have been thinking of an arrangement somewhat like the one worked out by the Sargent School in Boston (a college specializing in physical education for women) which was bequeathed to Boston University and despite becoming a part of the university, remained an identifiable unit. The date for Brown to collect on the offer was 1960, or Harry Jacob's death, whichever came sooner. If Brown declined, President Jacobs would be obliged to offer the school to another educational institution. (Everyone assumed that this clause referred to Providence College.) On April 30, 1949, the bill was passed by the Rhode Island legislature and thus Bryant became a non-profit institution governed by a board of trustees.[19] Bryant College ceased to be anyone's private property. The college was exempt from federal income taxes, but the state legislature held out for a few more years of property taxes and did not approve the state tax exemption until 1958.[20]

Brown University's president, Henry Wriston, did not quite know how a business school would fit into his university. He was a classicist, a believer in a traditional education, the last of a long line of ministers who had been heads of the university. Wriston hedged. Brown's next president, Barnaby Keeney, saw Bryant as a two-year college with a restricted program, too different from Brown—a four-year institution devoted to the liberal arts. In 1956, four years before the due date, he declined the offer once and for all, saying, "Brown and Bryant serve two different functions."[21] Providence College, under the leadership of another classicist, Father Robert Slavin, also declined. Publicly, Father Slavin said Bryant could do best as a separate college.[22]

At that point, an amendment to the original bill had to be passed stating that in 1960, Bryant College would be independent, not the property of Brown University or any other institution. Possibly, Harry Jacobs had counted on this turn of events. Certainly, Bryant College had much to gain in becoming tax-exempt.

The 1953 Class Day exercises were held on the lawn behind South Hall.

The new corporation, "The Bryant College of Business Admin-istration," paid Jacobs a sum (rumored to be $625,000 dollars) out of its operating funds over a ten-year period. Included in the settlement was an auditorium seating 700, classroom buildings, an administration building, buildings constructed for dormitories, and a gymnasium. Private resi-dences which Harry Jacobs had purchased for use as dormitories were leased by the college and were scheduled for purchase at a later date.[23] Nelson Gulski remarked of this financial deal, "He sold out at the top of the market!"[24] Harry Jacobs remained president, drawing a salary as well as the annual installment payments from the sale.

Always the shrewd business man, Jacobs decided in 1949 to hire a professional to handle the college's public relations. Both the elder Jacobs and his son Gardner were most adept at this, but Harry Jacobs wanted to project a new image for Bryant, one in keeping with its non-profit status. In the late forties, few colleges had such a position as director of public relations: advertising was frowned upon as a way of making educational institutions known. But Jacobs knew that Bryant and Stratton colleges had always put paid advertisements in newspapers and journals. Now he was concerned with image and he needed an expert in public relations who had an academic background and refinement in manner.[25]

He found just the right person in Gertrude Hochberg. She had majored in journalism in college and worked for a newspaper, had taken a position in advertising at Gimbel's department store in New York City, and a few years later had become advertising manager at Shepard's department store in Providence. When she went to Bryant for a job interview, she found to her surprise that Harry Jacobs "understood completely the principles of advertising."[26] She was hired the same day. The two made quite a pair. When the dignified, aging president arrived at the office in the morning, he said, "Good morning, Mrs. Barnum." She, bright-eyed and spritely, replied, "Good morning, Mr. Bailey."[27]

BRYANT COLLEGE CLASS DAY 1953

GRAY STUDIO PROV. R.I.

Gertrude Meth Hochberg became director of public relations for the college in 1949.

She became an important influence at the college because Harry Jacobs liked the image of Bryant she wanted to project.

Hochberg had graduated from an Ivy League school, but she had also lived through the Depression and knew how much it meant to prepare for a job and have an institution's help in getting one.[28] She set about publicizing the college with enthusiasm. She asked for the name and address of each student's hometown newspaper and high school paper. She then wrote an article on what the student was doing and sent it to his or her local publications, thereby securing free publicity for Bryant College in towns and schools all over the northeast. She had a talent for discovering human interest stories, and she was so good at writing that when she sent the local papers an article, they would often print it verbatim.[29]

She also wanted to publicize the faculty's expertise and willingness to use their knowledge in the service of the community. In the 1950s, Hochberg organized a radio program, "Bryant's View," which featured Bryant College faculty giving talks on practical financial problems such as, "How to Buy a House."[30] In 1952, a television series "Income Tax Information, Please" brought the college's faculty to the public's attention again.

Hochberg saw Bryant as a college in touch with the realities of the world outside academia. Accordingly, she believed that the college had to prepare its students for more than a business career, that educated men and women should also be leaders in areas other than the workplace. She supported Harry Jacobs in giving students more experiences in college life that would lead to consciousness of their lives as citizens. Jacobs began giving a Good Citizenship Award each year to the student who had gone out of the way to help others.[31] The school's motto, "Education For Business Leadership," took on a richer meaning.

In 1952 Hochberg and Jacobs gave enthusiastic support to students who formed an Interfaith Council and launched an annual Brotherhood Conference. Members of the Newman Club, the Canterbury Club, the Hillel Counselship, and the Bryant Christian Association worked to gain wide student participation in these conferences. Speaking to a meeting of the 1953 Brotherhood Conference, Jacobs said, "What I like best about this Brotherhood Week is that the idea comes from you." He went on to say, ". . . you demonstrate to all of us on this campus, to the members of the community, and to the world, that men can 'think apart and yet live together.' " He added, "This event transcends everything you do in the classroom; it gives a third dimension to your lives as students and is bound to have a profound influence on everything you do."[32]

Sylvia Porter was the financial editor of the New York Post when she received an honorary doctorate from Bryant in 1952.

Harry Jacobs and Gertrude Hochberg searched for ways to expand Bryant's contacts in the business community. To enable Bryant to play a role in the economic development of the state, they initiated the Business Management Institute in 1950. This became an annual service to the community which gave Bryant College publicity and visibility. The Providence Chamber of Commerce, the Rhode Island Port and Industrial Development Commission, and the Associated Industries of Rhode Island were among the groups participating. The focus was on assisting small industrial and retail businesses in solving management problems. The day-long conference usually began with an introductory

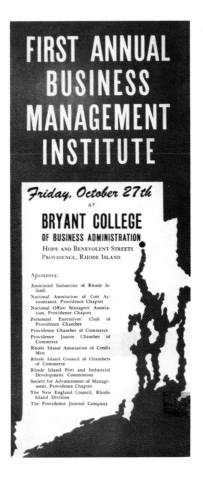

FIRST ANNUAL
BUSINESS
MANAGEMENT
INSTITUTE

Friday, October 27th
AT
BRYANT COLLEGE
OF BUSINESS ADMINISTRATION
HOPE AND BENEVOLENT STREETS
PROVIDENCE, RHODE ISLAND

Sponsors:

Associated Industries of Rhode Island.
National Association of Cost Accountants, Providence Chapter
National Office Managers' Association, Providence Chapter
Personnel Executives' Club of Providence Chamber
Providence Chamber of Commerce
Providence Junior Chamber of Commerce
Rhode Island Association of Credit Men
Rhode Island Council of Chambers of Commerce
Rhode Island Port and Industrial Development Commission
Society for Advancement of Management, Providence Chapter
The New England Council, Rhode Island Division
The Providence Journal Company

Harry Jacobs and Gertrude Hochberg started the Business Management Institute in 1950 to assist small businesses.

speech and case studies on crucial topics. Then, in the afternoon, there were panels and discussion groups. A bureau of research was started where students gained experience in conducting surveys and tabulating data; this important source of information was available for local businessmen.[33]

Harry Jacobs, always conscious of public relations, continued to make it his business to meet important people and make friends on his winter vacations in West Palm Beach, Florida. As he had done earlier with such success, he corresponded with individuals for a year or so, then offered the lure–an honorary degree–to get them to come to Bryant. In August 1944, Senate Majority Leader Alben Barkley spoke. In 1947, Secretary of the Treasury John Snyder received an honorary doctorate in business administration. Winthrop W. Aldrich, chairman of Chase National Bank of New York, also received an honorary degree.[34] In August 1949, the president of United States Steel, Benjamin F. Fairless, delivered the commencement address. Bryant's graduation made the national news because reporters covered the ceremony in hopes that Fairless would say something about the steel strike which was looming.[35] In the fifties, government leaders–Paul Douglas, United States Senator; Earl Jones McGrath, United States Commissioner of Education; and James P. Mitchell, Secretary of Labor– attended Bryant's graduation ceremonies as well as such famous businessmen as Mr. J. C. Penney.[36]

Oveta Culp Hobby, Secretary of Health, Education and Welfare, delivered the commencement address in 1953.

Graduation in 1953 was notable because it featured the first woman in Bryant's history to deliver the commencement address: Mrs. Oveta Culp Hobby, Secretary of the United States Department of Health, Education and Welfare. With her to receive an honorary degree was Ivy Baker Priest, the Treasurer of the United States.[37] Undoubtedly, this was the work of Gertrude Hochberg, who wanted role models for the women students at Bryant. From then on, women were the principal speakers from time to time, and women were chosen from various fields to be honored at commencement.

Gardner Jacobs described his father as a man whose greatest concern was to keep the college going, to keep it financially sound.[38] Harry Jacobs sought individuals who had practical experience in their particular area of business. He was not interested in advanced degrees. As for faculty, heavy teaching loads left them no time to pursue higher degrees or carry out research. They concentrated on doing a good job of teaching and took pride in preparing students for excellence in their future business careers.

As the decade of the 1950s went on, the elder Jacobs became more and more willing to leave the running of the school to his son, Gardner, then vice president, and two deans, Nelson Gulski and Lionel Mercier. Harry Jacobs' health declined. Often the chauffeur brought him to the college at ten o'clock in the morning and drove him home again at noon. His leaves during the winter months became longer. Although not officially president until 1961, Gardner Jacobs effectively headed the college beginning in the mid-fifties.[39]

As power gradually shifted from the elder Jacobs to the younger Jacobs, a change in direction was discernible. Gardner Jacobs said his vision was to build an institution that would endure.[40] Emphasis was no longer on profitability but on building academic programs that would ensure the college's future.

Gardner Jacobs was very much aware of developments in the field of education, and he began inching his reluctant father towards accepting the inevitable: Bryant College would have to gain accreditation. For decades Bryant had offered the kinds of courses that prepared students for jobs. Its accounting students consistently scored high in national examinations.[41] But when they wanted to go to graduate school, they found that the two-year degree did not include enough liberal arts courses to be acceptable. Also, graduate schools were wary of non-accredited colleges. Nelson Gulski commented: "While our people were welcomed in business, they were snubbed in academe."[42] Gardner Jacobs could see that the college would have to compete with four-year accredited institutions for students. If Bryant were to endure, changes in courses, calendar, and faculty credentials would have to be made and accreditation gained from the New England Association of Colleges and Secondary Schools.

In 1956 Gardner Jacobs directed administrators' efforts towards devising a three-year program of forty-four weeks of work per year. This included the prescribed percentage of liberal arts courses, according to

As Harry Jacobs's health declined, his son, Gardner Jacobs, began to take responsibility for running the college and finally became president in 1961.

accreditation standards.[43] He knew also that the small library at the corner of Hope and Benevolent Streets which the college had moved into in 1955 would be judged below standards. He began to search for a large structure near the college that he could convert to a library.

As Gardner Jacobs undertook these preparations, a debate was going on among professors and administrators. Some thought the college should do what it did best: prepare people in accounting and business administration. Others believed the college was correct in expanding its offerings so that students were educated for more aspects of their future lives than their jobs. Meanwhile, Gardner Jacobs went full steam ahead in planning the addition of liberal arts courses and people realized that eventually the number of required accounting and commercial law courses would be cut. At the end of the decade, both faculty and administrators were discussing and planning the specific liberal arts courses to be added, including laboratory science and advanced mathematics courses.[44]

Although the college had always been lenient in admitting students, standards for graduation were tough. This willingness to take a chance on a student meant that many people had the opportunity to go to the college. But in the mid-fifties, because of increasing numbers of applicants, Bryant became more selective in admitting students. There was a preparatory program for Korean War veterans, but the students had to do well to be admitted into a degree program.[45] By the end of the fifties, as Bryant prepared for accreditation, admissions standards were raised again, requiring good grades in high school.

Gardner Jacobs listened to ideas about improving programs. While he was not a lavish spender, he was willing to spend money when he was convinced the program was academically sound and financially viable. An example of this is the way he worked with Joseph Santos to improve the Evening Division. Santos, a practicing lawyer, came to Bryant in 1947 to teach commercial law. Five years later he became director of the Evening Division. Going through documents in the office and talking to people, he discovered that before World War II, the college had offered degrees in the Evening Division; however, so much attention had been placed on the double session during the day in the wartime era, the degree program at night had been phased out. Enrollment in the evening had dropped to a couple of hundred students.[46]

Santos found that students came to the Evening Division for a variety of reasons. Usually they were people who had jobs during the day and wanted to upgrade their credentials: bookkeepers came to learn accounting and thus expand their employment opportunities. Some came for special information they needed for the job they were in. One man, in his sixties, came in a chauffeur-driven limousine in order to stay informed of new developments in business. Others came to brush up on their knowledge of commercial law in order to pass the CPA examination. Santos was convinced that the Evening Division could also attract students who wanted and needed a college degree. There was only one other evening division in the state – the University of Rhode Island's – offering a degree in business at that time.[47]

Santos approached Gardner Jacobs with the aim of reorganizing Bryant's Evening Division so that it could grant degrees. Jacobs was skeptical at first, fearing that if a degree program were instituted, the college would lose money because it would have to offer courses with only marginal enrollment. Santos devised a program whereby there would be no required courses as such but there would be a required distribution. For many courses there was a logical sequence that could not be altered: a student had to take the first year of accounting before he could take the second. Santos argued that the system created enough flexibility for a degree program to be viable. Gardner Jacobs agreed.[48] The Evening Division announced in 1952 that a degree program had been instituted.[49] Soon the Evening Division was enrolling 400 students, and by the end of the decade – 500.

Santos also set out to expand Bryant's offerings so that the college could better serve adults from the community who needed financial information for their businesses. He always tried to get people at the top of a particular profession to teach special courses. For example, he would invite the top legal counsel in a major insurance company to teach a course for insurance underwriters. Often these experts were flattered to be asked and liked the opportunity to test their teaching skills and their knowledge. One of the most notable of these instructors was Frank Licht, a superior court judge (later governor of the state) who taught commercial law.[50] In 1954, when the federal internal revenue code was rewritten, Victor Pedorella, who had worked for the Internal Revenue Service for thirty years, offered a series of workshops for lawyers and accountants.[51] Santos especially wanted to help owners of small businesses, so he designed short, non-credit courses tailored to meet the needs of particular small firms. For example, one semester he offered a course for small restaurant owners featuring workshops on keeping records, calculating social security, and knowing the laws pertaining to the food business.[52]

In the 1950s, student services were not the large item in college budgets that they became in the seventies, but Bryant continued to put money and effort into the Placement Bureau. Under the direction of Lautrelle Love, the Placement Bureau honored its commitment to help every graduate find a job. Mrs. Love kept a confidential file on each student, and during the seniors' last semester, she met with each one privately. Employers contacted her, and she arranged job interviews, trying to match the graduate's interests and preferences to the potential employer's needs. She was determined to guide each student toward success. Underneath the charming manner of a Southern lady, she maintained an iron seriousness about this student service.

Another student service, financial aid, was in its infancy, however. In earlier decades, Gardner Jacobs had sought out students in need of financial aid and on an informal basis offered the students a partial remission of tuition costs as well as help getting part-time jobs at the college or nearby in the city. There were few scholarships. In 1939, the alumni set up a special fund to give $100 scholarships to ten students per year. The state regularly granted a number of partial scholarships for high school graduates who wanted to complete the business teacher-training degree and teach in Rhode Island's public schools. The Harriet E. Jacobs Memorial Award, set up by her family, enabled the college to give a full tuition scholarship to a student of high academic ability. Other small awards, given for academic excellence at graduation time, were of great psychological benefit to the graduating senior but did not help the undergraduate struggling financially to stay in school.

In 1959, however, financial assistance came of age. Russia's success with its scientific program was dramatically demonstrated by the launching of the satellite Sputnik. This prompted the United States Congress to provide for the national defense by granting student loans. The intent was to train future teachers, primarily in the sciences. At the end of the fifties, these government loans made a Bryant education accessible to a number of students.

Thus, the growth in Bryant's student body, begun at the end of the forties with World War II veterans attending under the G.I. Bill and continued by Korean War veterans in the early fifties, was now sustained by students supported by government loans. Most students were working-class and the first in their families to go to college. Although students were predominantly New Englanders, the Bryant population showed a wide geographic diversity with twenty-eight states and ten foreign countries represented.

In spite of the increase in the number of students and faculty, there was still a sense at Bryant of belonging to a community. Classes had fifty or more students, but Bryant faculty still prided themselves on their individualistic approach to students.[53] Each paper had to be carefully graded, each question answered, each person's needs considered.

There were some strains within the family, of course. Some students took the bus (streetcars had disappeared from Providence by the end of the forties), but many drove their own cars. Finding a parking space was a daily struggle. Students would park on Hope Street. The police would chalk the tires; students would run out during the break between classes and move their cars forward enough to hide the chalk marks, and the game went on. Sometimes a desperate student parked in an equally desperate faculty member's space, and the ensuing confrontation reached the heights of drama.[54]

Beginning in the 1950s, Bryant fraternities became involved in a variety of community projects.

Several fraternities caused the college administrators and students annoyance, and in some cases, there was danger to life and property during hazing week. This was a nationwide phenomenon which Bryant did not escape. But Bryant students sought social action programs for their fraternities and sororities.[55] Fraternities initiated "charitable hazing": one sent pledges to rake leaves for Butler Hospital, and another white-washed basement walls for Providence Hebrew Day School. Each year, one group presented under-privileged children with a Christmas party. Another took children on an annual picnic. A total of 23 projects involved 289 students.[56]

People at Bryant remembered the easy acceptance that students in the 1950s accorded each other. Dominic Falcone '50 summed up the feeling: "Everyone was equal."[57] Still, Bryant College could not escape the Cold War atmosphere of the McCarthy era. In 1950 the president of the student senate, who was said to be a communist, was ousted from his office and forced to leave the college.[58]

As a whole, however, the fifties were years of bustle and optimism when few questions were asked about society and education. Most students did what was expected of them and conformed to rules without protest. The chief rule for men was no alcoholic beverages in the rooms. Proper dress was required in the dining room: men came to dinner in coats and ties, women in dresses, hose, and heels. There were no curfews for men, but women had to be in their dormitories by 10:00 on week nights and 11:00 on weekends. Any woman leaving the dormitory in the evening had to sign out, with time and destination noted, and sign in on returning. Women students had to leave the library at 9:45 to get back to their dormitory by 10:00, while their male peers stayed to study another hour.[59] Occasionally, a little flame of rebellion flickered and a latecomer to the dormitory would climb dexterously up the fire escape.[60]

In each dormitory, the elected president and counselors constituted a house council which established the rules. However, there were limits defined by the housemothers; the dean of women, Philomena Castronovo; and the dean of men, William Fales. The house council reviewed cases of infractions of the rules, but serious matters were taken up by a committee consisting of Dean Fales, Dean Castronovo, Dean of the College Nelson Gulski, and the president of the student senate.

Social life on campus was fairly staid. There were teas to which the women students came dressed up, including white gloves, and where Dean Castronovo and the housemother formed a receiving line. Dean Castronovo saw these exercises as teaching social graces which would transfer to the business world in the graduate's later life.[61]

There were many regularly scheduled activities. The honor society – called the Key Society – brought together students who excelled in academics. Professional clubs, such as the Business Administration Society, the Teacher-Training Society, the Accountancy and Finance Society, and the Advertising Club, helped students learn the formal and informal requirements of their chosen fields. Cultural clubs, especially the Literary Club and the International Relations Club, gave them an opportunity to widen their interests. The college drama club, "The Masquers," continued to stage plays in the Bryant auditorium. There was a paid instructor for the athletic program which included intramural bowling, softball, and basketball leagues. Men's varsity sports teams, such as basketball and baseball, which had existed in the 1930s but had been suspended during World War II and the Korean War, were reinstated in the mid-fifties. These teams competed against college and amateur sports teams in southeastern New England, and varsity basketball gave Bryant its first taste of regular media attention.[62] The Student Senate, whose membership included one representative from each fraternity, sorority, residence hall, and from every organization on campus, coordinated college activities.

College life in the 1950s included formal teas, visits to the soda fountain, and wearing beanies during freshman week. Above, President and Mrs. Harry Jacobs attend the 1955 mother-daughter tea. Opposite, freshmen serenade coeds in front of Salisbury Hall.

Fraternities and sororities sponsored Saturday night dances, all reported on in glowing terms in the student paper now called *The Archway*. Homecoming Week was always a notable occasion. In 1957 it began with a special lunch at the college cafeteria and proceeded with the President's Reception on the Green, the Greek Letter Hot Dog Roast at the athletic field, a social hour at the student union, a homecoming banquet in the new college refectory, and dancing in the auditorium.[63] On a day-to-day basis, students had their favorite hangouts, like Bovie's, where they had a beer, watched television, and danced.

The work week of the commuting students offered little time for social activities, however. Their lifestyle tended to be one of study, part-time jobs, and long commutes. Student Karl Ericson (later chairman of the board of trustees), a veteran of four years in the navy, drove an hour from Connecticut each day to attend Bryant. He worked hours each week as a butcher to put himself through college. He did take time to attend one dance and there met his future wife, Jacquelyn Ruest.[64] A future professor of business administration, Clarissa Patterson, then a young woman training to be a secretarial studies teacher, commuted from Foster, took a full load of courses, worked part-time at the college, had a job at Brown, and on the weekends, worked in a grocery store. (She still found time to be assistant editor of *The Archway*.)[65] Another lifestyle for Bryant students was represented by Frank Delmonico (later vice president for financial affairs), who was also a veteran. He had a liberal arts degree, a bank job, and a family. He went to Bryant at night for five years to get his degree in accounting and business administration. Delmonico worked all day, went to class in the evenings, and studied all day Sundays. (Saturdays were reserved for family outings and work around the house.)[66]

In the last few years of the decade, the college once again embarked on expansion. In 1956, Harry Jacobs began construction of a two-story colonial style brick building on Young Orchard Avenue. The first floor offered classroom space. The second floor contained a dining hall with the capacity to seat 420, a faculty dining room, and a kitchen. The old cafeteria became a student union, with snack bar and television lounge. The second floor of the union was outfitted as a game room with ping pong and shuffleboard. Gardner Jacobs worked out the designs with the architects for the new building and renovation of the old.[67]

Gardner Jacobs was determined to build a men's dormitory so that male students would have good housing and would not have to feel crowded in college residences or seek boarding houses or rooms off campus. He hated the idea of borrowing money to build, but the need was undeniable. Probably for the first time, Bryant administrators became aware of external sources that could be tapped, and Gardner Jacobs made up his mind to seek federal assistance. He went to Washington to inquire about the fund for loans to colleges which needed additional student housing. In Washington he talked to a government official, Ralph Cornell, at the Department of Housing and Urban Development, who by a lucky circumstance knew about Bryant College. Cornell said that the fund had nearly run out, that he had only two million dollars left. "Great!" replied Gardner Jacobs. When Cornell asked whether the board of trustees had approved a loan, Gardner Jacobs admitted, "I can't lie to you. They haven't approved it, but you just hold it until tomorrow morning. I'll get their approval."[68]

Jacobs had to get to the airport quickly and fly to New York to work out the details with the regional director before the office closed on Friday. Over the weekend he was back in Rhode Island, calling all the trustees to get approval for the loan. Earlier in the college's history, Harry Jacobs had told the board whatever he was going to do, and they had routinely given him a vote of approval. With his son, the trustees still gave the expected assent, but Gardner Jacobs tended to take more time explaining and earning their permission before he carried out an action. They heartily approved this loan. On Monday morning he was in New York, ready to sign the $874,000 loan agreement.[69]

The new dormitory, a structure built on Power Street, enabled the college to provide attractive and convenient housing for men. Women benefited too, since other residences formerly used for men could now be renovated for them. The East Side college, with its brand new buildings, looked impressive.

Looking back on the late forties and the fifties, it is clear that increasing numbers of students compelled the college to expand its facilities. Other changes, less tangible but of crucial importance, were going on as well. Bryant ceased to be a proprietary institution and gained non-profit status. The primary goal shifted from financial profitability to academic programs that would ensure the college's future. Gardner Jacobs began to move the college towards accreditation by an outside agency, the New England Association of Colleges and Secondary Schools. And the college's chief administrator went to the federal government for a loan.

In the past, the external world had affected Bryant College, especially in the form of national events such as changes in office technology or world wars. However, the college had remained inward-looking. Now, at the end of the 1950s, people connected with Bryant assumed the college had every right to the respect of the world outside and to the advantages other colleges gained from federal agencies.

In the late 1950s, Harry Jacobs's career as an educator was nearing its end. The college was changing dramatically. By 1960 it had officially become a non-profit institution and Jacobs had sold the college buildings and land to the corporation.

The 1960s: Revolutionary Changes

IN 1961, Harry Jacobs, now eighty-six years old, accepted the title of president emeritus and formally relinquished the power that had been slipping away as his absences became longer during the last years of the 1950s. The trustees unanimously elected the sixty-year-old Gardner Jacobs president. He had been vice president for thirty years and looking back on that time, he quipped, "I had had enough of vice."[1]

Harry Jacobs, still very much saddened by the death of his wife, Jeannette Carroll Jacobs, in 1956, put his fine business mind to work on "eternal success." He told Henry Foley that he had "covered all the bases"–he had left provisions in his will for Jewish, Catholic, and Protestant charities.[2] He died in January 1963. There were former students and teachers all over the country–dating from graduates of the Rhode Island Commercial School in 1910–who mourned his death. The Rhode Island legislature voted a resolution noting his contributions to the state. Not only had he been an educator, but he had given his time freely to the community, serving on the boards of both schools and hospitals.

Harry Jacobs' death coincided with the beginning of revolutionary changes at the college. In the early sixties, accreditation put Bryant on a new level vis-à-vis other New England colleges. In the mid- and late-1960s, two events profoundly altered Bryant's history: unionization of the faculty and student rebellion. As the decade closed, the acquisition of the campus in Smithfield gave the college a new life.

The sixties began with the first visit of the accrediting team from the New England Association of Colleges and Secondary Schools. It inspected the campus and programs in 1961 and decided to recommend accreditation. However, the Association's officers turned Bryant down. Undaunted, Gardner Jacobs organized visits to other campuses and talked to administrators about optimum facilities and techniques in accredited business education programs. He went to Northeastern University and the Massachusetts Institute of Technology to talk to presidents there (both of whom were his personal friends) and sought their frank advice about what he should do to prepare the college for accreditation.[3] He learned that he would have to build up the library's holdings, institute faculty committees to share in college governance, upgrade the faculty (as far as degrees were concerned), and increase the liberal arts offerings so that half of the students' courses would be in liberal arts.

In 1961, Bryant boasted an extensive campus abutting Brown University on College Hill. Gardner Hall is the large building at left center. South Hall, above Gardner Hall, is accentuated by the archway at the right end. Jacobs Hall is to the right of South Hall; the Administration Building and Kilcup Hall are to the left.

Gardner Jacobs set out to follow these recommendations. Checking on colleges accredited by the New England Association of Colleges and Secondary Schools, he found that three-year schools had little chance of gaining accreditation.[4] The college community accepted the inevitability of the traditional four-year academic calendar, and the college switched over. (An associate's degree continued to be given for the two-year secretarial program.) By giving up the shortened time schedule, the college relinquished one of the main advantages it had offered students in the past. Jacobs believed that the students would gain, however, because their degree would be from an accredited institution.

Jacobs bought a huge mansion at 128 Hope Street in 1961 and converted it to a library. The next year he built a wing which provided an additional 5,000 square feet of space. Efforts to further increase the library's holdings were stepped up.

Jacobs ordered faculty committees to be set up, and they were organized; but they met only a few times a year and then just to receive information. The most important change was to come in the curriculum because of the increase in the number of liberal arts courses: the 50–50 ratio of liberal arts to business courses was not yet a reality but it was the goal faculty worked towards. It became possible now for students to major in business, but concentrate their electives in a chosen liberal arts field.

In 1964 Bryant College achieved the accreditation it sought from the New England Association of Colleges and Secondary Schools. Gardner Jacobs had the letter granting accreditation framed and mounted on the wall. Whenever he passed it, he saluted, saying, "You cost us a million bucks!"[5]

No one doubted that the cost was offset by the advantages. Now Bryant's graduates were acceptable to graduate schools. The college could compete with other business colleges for the best students. And faculty benefited because the administration reduced the teaching load from twenty-one to fifteen hours. With this improvement the college could more easily attract qualified faculty. Furthermore, Bryant, as an

Bryant's quest for accreditation in the 1960s necessitated improved library facilities. A former residence at 128 Hope Street became the library in 1961. A new wing was added a year later.

accredited college, stood a better chance of receiving grants from foundations and government agencies.

Excellence in specific programs also received recognition. In 1966, Bryant's teacher education program was awarded national accreditation, and Bryant became a member of the American Association of Colleges for Teacher Education.[6] Professor Priscilla Moulton Phillips directed the teacher education program with the goal of keeping it ahead of technological developments in business.

The Bryant College campus continued to expand in the sixties as it had in the fifties. Gardner Jacobs eagerly searched for ways to gain more space. In a dedication ceremony in December 1960, Ernest Kilcup, chairman of the board of trustees, presented Gardner Jacobs with the keys to a brand new building, Gardner Hall. In 1961, the new classroom building, Kilcup Hall, was begun with a bequest from the late board chairman. Shortly afterwards, Jacobs purchased a Charlesfield Street apartment house (located across the street from Memorial Hall) and began renovation of it for use as a men's dormitory. In 1964, he bought a large house at 26 Cooke Street and in the same year began construction of a wing to Memorial Hall. The next year, a new men's dormitory was begun. Gardner Jacobs very happily promised that a new and much larger Bryant College would welcome students when they came back in September 1965.[7]

While the campus expanded physically, Bryant's bureaucracy also grew. In July 1961, the Student Activities Office was separated from the Alumni Office, and the college acquired a full-time director of alumni affairs in Kenneth Cedergren '57. Robert Hathaway, Jr. '49, became director of student activities.

The latter office supervised a variety of activities including cultural events and the athletic program. Maurice Clare, who worked there as a student helper in the early sixties and then came back in 1967 as assistant director, said, "If there were a group that was really interested in doing something and we thought there'd be a lot of involvement, we found some money here and there to assist them."[8]

Intramural sports were popular: Clare estimated that over 40 percent of the students participated in at least one activity. Volleyball was a favorite and Clare, along with athletic directors from the fraternities and leaders of the independents' teams, organized two volleyball leagues. In addition, there were teams in softball, badminton, basketball, bowling, horse shoe pitching, table tennis, and touch football. Clare started the first girls' basketball team in 1964.[9]

At the beginning of the sixties, the varsity basketball team was coached by Professor Wallace Camper. Intramural competition was far more popular than varsity sports, and Camper had to persuade the college's top players to play for the varsity team when both intramural and varsity games were scheduled on the same night. But interest grew and in 1964 the administration hired Tom Duffy, an outstanding coach and teacher in the Pawtucket, Rhode Island, public school system, to coach varsity basketball. The next year Bryant's Indians won the Naismith Conference championship and for three years after that were conference champions. The year 1966–67 was the best season for the Indians in Bryant history: they won 22 out of 24 games. For several weeks, the team's star, Tom Smile from Pawtucket, was the leading scorer in the nation with a 30-plus per game average. In 1967, Bryant was voted a member of the National Collegiate Athletic Association, the national governing body of intercollegiate athletics.[10]

Varsity teams in baseball, track and field, golf, and tennis were organized on student demand.[11] These teams had faculty coaches. In 1968, Duffy gave up coaching, and Bryant searched for a professional coach for basketball. Within a year Bryant acquired its first full-time athletic director, Tom Folliard. The commitment of the faculty coaches, the dedication of Folliard, and the energy and enthusiasm of the students, meant that Bryant usually played well. Soon the teams and their coaches realized they had made a name for themselves. Maurice Clare said, "Whenever we travelled, we got a lot of respect—people knew about Bryant College."[12]

The campus offered more cultural activities in the sixties than it had in earlier decades. The lecture committee brought four distinguished speakers to the campus each year. The drama group, the Masquers, continued to be active, and the club was greatly encouraged by the real stage it acquired in the new student union. Students belonged to a number of other clubs, as well. The World Affairs Forum, advised by Professor Sol Lebovitz from the political science department, was especially active. Members represented the college at the 1967 National Model General Assembly in New York. The college glee club, the Bryant Choralaires, under the direction of Professor Richard Alberg, added zest to special occasions; and students were proud to have their own dance band, the Stardusters.

While student activities were growing in number, tuition fees were increasing due to inflation, and the matter of financial aid was becoming more complicated. Tuition regularly increased by about $100 a year in the early sixties; by 1966 it was $1,100. In 1967, it jumped by $150 to reach a total of $1,250 a year, and in 1969 tuition was hiked up by $200 to $1,450.[13] Students were confronted with the necessity of taking out larger and larger loans. (Students in previous decades would have been shocked by these costs.) However, outside aid in the form of alumni scholarships also increased. The college received a windfall in 1965 when the Office of Education began giving it an annual grant for work-study.

In 1966, responding to students' needs, Bryant hired a full-time [aid director, Thom Brown.[14] Bryant also administered the Nation Defense Student Loan Program and the Educational Opportunity (The latter had to be matched by the college's contributions. This w beginning of a continuous increase in financial aid by the college itsen.

In 1963 Bryant College celebrated its one-hundredth birthday. As part of the celebration, Gertrude Hochberg wanted to demonstrate Bryant's interest in women's professional lives which she saw as a continuous theme in the college's history going back to the founder, E. W. Mason. Soberly she surveyed the situation: the college's auditorium on Hope Street would hold only 400 people. She decided Bryant would present a symposium and invite the area's four hundred most influential women. The topic would be drawn from President John F. Kennedy's commissioned report, "The Status of Women in America," which had just been completed. Hochberg had to battle to convince male administrators and faculty that this was a good idea. She argued that there were seven male students to every female student on the Bryant campus and that the college needed to do something spectacular to attract the attention of young women.[15]

Hochberg proceeded to invite Esther Peterson, Assistant Secretary of Labor and the chairperson of President Kennedy's commission, to preside over the symposium. Panel discussions were led by women from business, politics, education, civic groups, religion, and medicine. The participants considered such issues as equal rights and privileges for women, equal job opportunities, and pay scales. They also pondered questions such as, "How can a woman maintain her traditional role of mother and house manager and yet actively participate in business?"[16] Articulation of these issues at such an early date put Bryant way ahead of the times. Recognizing Bryant's leadership in this social movement, Governor John Chafee invited Hochberg to form the Rhode Island Commission on the Status of Women.

Part of the centennial celebration in 1963, Bryant's symposium, "The Status of Women in America," was chaired by Esther Peterson, Assistant Secretary of Labor in the Kennedy administration. (Left to right are Jessie Bernard of Pennsylvania State University, Pauli Murray of Yale Law School, Esther Peterson and Marion Stephenson, vice-president of NBC.)

The centennial celebration included a Civil War-era costume ball (above, students Kathy Carroll and Ron Tsolis) and a ceremonial flag raising. (Left to right are Jane Eaton, a member of the Bryant Pep Club; Robert Cabral; Thomas Taylor; Bill Word, president of the student senate; and Robert Hathaway, director of student activities. Danny O'Connell, president of the Greek Letter Council, raised the flag with assistance from Bill Word.)

Throughout the year, many famous people came to the campus to speak. For the centennial lecture, G. Mennen Williams, Assistant Secretary of State for African Affairs and former Michigan governor, spoke on the problems of the new nations of Africa. The French Consul General in Boston, M. Jean Savelli, spoke on "France and the Common Market." The occasion was well attended—tangible evidence of Bryant teachers' and students' interest in international business and the global economy.

On Bryant's initiative, Rhode Island's business teachers met on campus to discuss "New Horizons in Business Education." The event demonstrated the college's continuing leadership in the area of teacher education.[17]

That year's convocation featured John E. Fogarty, a congressman from Rhode Island. Delegates from learned and professional societies and from eighty colleges and universities—ranging from Harvard University, founded in 1636, to the Massachusetts Bay Community College, founded in 1961—attended the convocation to honor Bryant College.[18] The anniversary ended in December with a gala event, the Centennial Ball.[19]

In the summer of 1963 students and alumni from Bryant College boarded the SS France for forty-one days in Western Europe. Professor Wallace Camper organized the tour so that students could learn about international trade and European businesses. He arranged for heads of banks, businesses, unions, and government ministries to explain how their offices functioned and answer questions from Bryant students. He had made all travel arrangements: the cost to each participant was

Senator Claiborne Pell (center) and Marion Stephenson, vice president of NBC, participated in the centennial commencement. Rhode Island Governor John Chafee (below) gave the address.

Many congratulatory messages were sent to the college during its 100th year including this telegram from John F. Kennedy dated November 18, 1963.

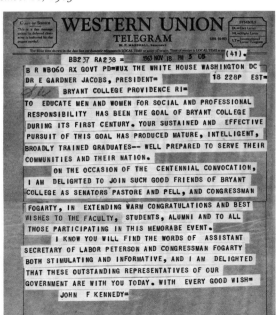

$1,100 – this included all travel, hotels, meals, and the sight-seeing on the itinerary. The administration was skeptical and refused to fund the project, so Camper took out a loan so that the students could go. They met representatives from such organizations as the European Common Market, the British Federation of Industries, the British Trades Union Congress, Lloyd's of London, the Netherlands Economic Ministry, the German Ministry of Finance, Daimler-Benz Corporation, Olivetti Business Machines Company, the Swiss Credit Bank, the Italian Foreign Ministry, and the International Labour Organization.[20] They also visited historic sites and attended cultural events. At Bryant the next fall, Secretary-Treasurer Ray Appleby gave Camper a check to cover the rest of the loan.[21] College administrators were convinced this was a valuable learning experience for students. In subsequent years, every week in the spring semester students attended a lecture on the organizations they would come in contact with on the European tour. After the tour, they wrote a paper on their research and received three hours of course credit.

While physical expansion and innovations such as the European study trip were going on, several revolutions were also in the making. Faculty had expected the accreditation process to bring them some power in decision-making, but it had not. The committees were on the books, but they had no power. Faculty knew their counterparts at other colleges did participate in committees with power to affect decisions on curriculum and tenure.

There was no such thing as tenure at Bryant, however. An individual negotiated with the college administration each year and was hired on an annual basis. Many of the faculty members had progressed into middle age while teaching at Bryant and looked back on twenty or thirty years of service to the college. They felt a very close identification with Bryant, but they had no guarantee they would be there the next year.

Their awareness of this uncertainty was heightened by the fact that administrators had to upgrade faculty credentials in order to achieve and retain accreditation. Now people with Ph.D.s were preferred, with anyone holding less than a master's not even considered for a teaching position. Of the eighty faculty members and administrators then at Bryant, fourteen had Ph.D.s and thirty-seven had master's degrees. The rest had undergraduate degrees only.[22] In the past, faculty had taught so many hours a week and so many students (fifty to sixty per class), that it was impossible for anyone to work on obtaining a higher degree. There had been no faculty development programs to pay faculty to take a year's leave to work toward a degree and no such thing as a sabbatical.

Finally, the faculty witnessed a series of demotions during preparation for accreditation. College administrators had been casual about titles in the past.[23] Now full professors without master's degrees became associate professors or even assistant professors.

Habitual ways of doing things—left-overs from the decades early in the century when Bryant was a business school and not a college—persisted. Often these seemed demeaning to the faculty. One such procedure was recounted by Frank Delmonico, who earned his degree in business administration at Bryant and returned to the college as assistant bursar in 1964. One Friday he accompanied Secretary-Treasurer Ray Appleby to the faculty dining room where Delmonico witnessed an event that caused him considerable embarrassment. Each faculty member came up to Appleby and waited while he peeled off a check and handed it over. The image of a professor holding out his hand for his pay stayed with Delmonico. When he became paymaster, he arranged to have the checks put in an envelope. Faculty could choose to pick them up in the faculty dining room, stop by the business office, or have them mailed.[24]

As for salaries, each faculty member negotiated individually with the dean of his division. If the teacher felt reluctant to accept what was given, the administrator might indicate that he or she could look elsewhere for a job. One year faculty were informed that money was tight and that they should accept the fact there would be no salary increase. They did so "in the family spirit," according to the administration. Faculty jokingly referred to themselves as "the living endowment."[25] Because of their low salaries, faculty felt they were subsidizing the college.

Faculty morale was low: possibly this was one of the reasons Jacobs and the board of trustees hired a firm, Knight and Gladieux Management Consultants, to advise them on ways to improve the work environment. The firm observed, "Dissatisfaction is also evident with respect to teaching loads and salaries, crowded offices not conducive to student counseling, lack of secretarial assistance in lesson and test preparation, and the requirement that faculty assist in the manual preparation of student schedules."[26] The firm told Jacobs and the board that departments should be better organized and the role of department chairs should be clarified and strengthened. The general conclusion of this report was that greater participation of the faculty in decision-making at the college was needed. Bernard Gladieux summed up the firm's observations in a letter to Gardner Jacobs: "As you know from our draft report, we have been critical of Bryant's historical tendency to treat its faculty more as employees in a business sense than as honored professionals."[27] The report was filed, but no action was taken.

In April 1967, one incident proved to be the catalyst for the faculty to take action. Parking around campus was a major problem for everyone, but faculty usually had space assigned to them. One day Associate Professor of History James Ingraham drove to his accustomed parking place only to find it occupied. Upon inquiring at the office, he found that it had been given to a secretary. He felt this was typical of the way professors were treated. The weight of the grievances that had piled up over the years bore down. "My soul is outraged!" he declared to President Jacobs.[28]

Ingraham went down to "The Hole"—a smoking area for male faculty members in the basement of South Hall. (It was dark and sparsely furnished, shaped like a railway car with chairs down two walls, and so had acquired this name.) When Ingraham recounted what had just happened, other faculty members there were also outraged over the incident. They agreed that some kind of collective action was the answer.[29]

Two years earlier, Wallace Camper had tried to form a chapter of the American Association of University Professors and had called a meeting that all the faculty attended. But college administrators had told him to drop it. Gardner Jacobs had pointed out that since Camper did not have a master's degree, he could be fired on that point alone. When Camper persisted, he found that few faculty members returned membership cards.[30] Clearly, the AAUP was not an alternative.

Henry Foley remarked, "Looks like we'll have to join some kind of union."[31] No one knew how to go about doing this. James Ingraham went to the telephone and called the Providence office of the AFL-CIO.

A week later James Ingraham, Albert McAloon, Wallace Camper, Herbert McLaughlin, Henry Foley, and Cornelius McAuliffe met Miles Holmes, the business representative of unionized school teachers (American Federation of Teachers) in Rhode Island. He advised them to find out whether their fellow faculty members really wanted a union by submitting a petition and cards for them to sign. Holmes reminded them that institutions of higher education were not covered in the laws governing the National Labor Relations Board and that they would not have the protection of the law. Henry Foley and James Ingraham went around to faculty members' homes that

Prof. James Ingraham explains faculty concerns to a reporter. The faculty union at Bryant was the first in the United States to achieve collective bargaining.

evening. They found that some colleagues declined—they were afraid of losing their jobs or else they felt that as professionals, they should not belong to a union. However, the majority signed. Armed with these signatures, they secured a charter from the American Federation of Labor to establish Local 1769.[32]

At the college, administrators were surprised at this turn of events. Dean Gulski asked Henry Foley to come to his office. "What's wrong?" he asked. Foley explained that faculty wanted to participate in decisions affecting themselves and the future of the college.[33] Gardner Jacobs was especially shocked. Apparently he did not see salaries at Bryant as the "disaster" the faculty believed they were. He remarked, "If you pay decent salaries and grant reasonable requests, you won't have a need for a union."[34] When a delegation of thirty faculty members asked to see him, he refused. They followed him home and knocked on his door, rang bells, and raised a clatter. He still refused. Nearly two weeks went by. Faculty decided to withhold their final semester grades until the president agreed to talk to them.[35]

Faculty members felt affection for Gardner Jacobs. They knew he was a well-meaning person. They were aware, too, that he was the one man at the college who represented continuity with the past—going back to 1916 when his father bought the old Bryant and Stratton.[36] The confrontation was as painful for them as it was for Gardner Jacobs. However, Jacobs had never been inflexible and his tendency was to listen. In its May 12, 1967, meeting, the

Gardner Jacobs presided over a sometimes rebellious faculty and student body until he relinquished the presidency in 1969 to concentrate on fundraising as chancellor of the college.

board of trustees discussed the matter and authorized the president to hold elections by secret ballot to ascertain the wishes of the faculty.[37] Jacobs told Ingraham that he would meet a faculty committee on May 17. Ingraham designated the entire faculty a committee, and they all crowded into the meeting room. Jacobs stated that his door was always open, that everyone at Bryant was in one big family, and that he had always wanted to work with the faculty to improve the college. He ended by saying, "I'll give you whatever you want." Ingraham replied, "We want a union."[38]

Jacobs insisted that an election by secret ballot would have to be held so that he could be certain that a union was truly desired by the faculty. In the ensuing election on May 19, union supporters won 35 to 20. Bryant's was the first faculty union in a four-year college in the United States to achieve collective bargaining.[39]

Immediately, the effects of unionization began to be felt. James Ingraham was elected president of the union on May 23, 1967, and the faculty also elected a negotiating team to work on a contract. Their major concerns in this first contract were tenure and salary.

Herbert McLaughlin, a professor of law, wrote the tenure policy, basing it on the Boston University policy, and submitted it as part of the first contract.[40] After serving for three years, any associate or full professor appointed for a fourth year received tenure; any instructor or assistant professor who had served for five years and received a contract for the sixth year received tenure. These provisions were applied to all full-time faculty serving in May 1967. If, in the future, reappointment were denied, the faculty member would be granted a hearing by an elected faculty committee.

To figure out what the salaries should be, faculty members filed into a room and put their paychecks on the table. It was the first time there had been such open discussion on what individuals were paid. People were surprised. Women were being paid much less than men.[41] Some full professors were making less than assistant professors.[42] Now the faculty set minimums for each rank and requested an across-the-board raise for every faculty member of $1,500.[43]

Faculty then turned their attention to such matters as course load and teaching conditions. Course load was reduced from fifteen to twelve hours and thus was brought into line with the load faculty carried at other colleges. It was stipulated that the size of lecture classes could not exceed fifty students. The faculty also decided that never again would they do the record-keeping tasks at the end of the semester. Such tasks were clerical and not academic, they declared.[44] The administration agreed to these provisions.

A restructuring of the college, accomplished by a series of formal agreements, took place during the year following the first contract. Changes were incorporated in the new faculty manual which John LaFontaine wrote. The former system wherein the two deans, Nelson Gulski and Lionel Mercier, made the major decisions was replaced by a system of shared governance by administrators and faculty committees. By December 1967, agreement had been reached on two important committees. First, the Committee on Faculty Rank and Appointment made recommendations on appointments, salaries, promotions, and release of faculty members. The recommendations were subject to the approval of the vice president for academic affairs, but if he took action contrary to the committee's decision, he had to justify his decision in a letter to the president. If the president supported him, he had to explain his reasons to the committee which could then appeal to the board of trustees. Only the three faculty members on the committee could vote; however, the college president and the vice president for academic affairs sat on the committee as non-voting members. The Curriculum Committee was set up along the lines described above for the Committee on Faculty Rank and Appointment.[45]

Academic departments, which had been loosely gathered together in April 1967 and existed in name but without power, now became organized under chairs who did have power. For example, the chair recommended the hiring of a new member of the department. If the department voted to support his or her recommendation, it was forwarded it to the Committee on Faculty Rank and Appointment and from there, it was sent to the vice president for academic affairs.[46]

James Ingraham said that the new faculty committees moved the college in the general direction that Gardner Jacobs wanted—in the direction of modernization. This meant that the institution now had a broader base of support because a greater number of its people participated in decisions affecting it. In the Declaration of the Bryant Faculty Federation, Ingraham summed up the intent of the changes:

> Bryant has become a professional college. Its objective is to provide, not merely instruction in business procedures, but a learning environment within which the student can mature to the threshold of a professional life. Insofar as maturity requires individual freedom, it occurs only in an environment that seeks originality and personal responsibility, which are the fundamental ingredients of freedom. To create this environment, the faculty must be independent. Teachers must be individuals acting in accordance with their own professional authority, enjoying the self-government previously enjoyed only by administrators.[47]

The result of these changes was that faculty felt increased self-respect. There was a general lifting of morale. Faculty manifested the new attitude by creating new courses and by taking advantage of the subsidies in tuition and books the college now offered to those willing to return to graduate school to complete higher degrees.[48]

AMA

Thursday, January 11th

Admiral Inn

Cumberland, R. I.

6:00 to 9:00 P.M.

Speaker

Mr. Joseph M. Hinchey

The Archway

Published by the Undergraduates of Bryant College, Providence, R. I.

TONIGHT

BRYANT

VS.

NICHOLS

8:00 P.M.

Vol. XXVIII, No. #/#   Wednesday, January 10, 196

Beta Iota Beta Becomes Affiliate Of Tau Kappa Epsilon

The Brothers of Beta Iota Beta are very proud to announce that as of December 21, 1967, we have become a recognized affiliate of Tau Kappa Epsilon National Fraternity.

Tau Kappa Epsilon was founded in 1899 at Illinois Wesleyan University and has grown to 234 active chapters where it stands as the largest college social fraternity. With its 10,000 undergraduate members and 62,000 living alumni, TKE is ranked 7th in "quality" (of the 60 national fraternities) by an independent College Survey Bureau.

We feel that TKE's reputation for help and guidance to its chapters, its Leadership Schools for chapters, its Scholarship and House Funds, its Employment Placement Service, and its non restrictive membership clauses should help to bring about in our brotherhood

an organization approaching the ultimate in fraternity life at Bryant. TKE representatives are already helping us plan for life on the new campus.

As an affiliate of Tau Kappa Epsilon the brothers and future pledges of BIB retain, for the present, their name, activities, constitution, and by-laws. However, the members of BIB will start to use TKE materials for rushing, as well as TKE manuals in pledging and every day operations. This affiliation period will last until Beta Iota Beta completes certain requirements which include submitting a lengthy formal petition. But they expect to be fully chaptered by May or early next fall at the latest.

BIB hopes this National affiliation with Tau Kappa Epsilon will benefit Beta Iota Beta, the Greek Letter Council, and Bryant College.

Union Signs Major Policy-Making Agreement

As a result of an agreement made between the Bryant Faculty Federation and the Bryant College administration on the 19th of December, 1967, two new committees have been officially recognized as major academic policy-making organs of Bryant College. The two committees are (1) The Committee on Faculty Rank and Appointment, and (2) the Curriculum Committee. Each committee is composed of representatives from both the Faculty and the Administration.

The Committee on Faculty Rank and Appointment is responsible for considering appointments, salaries, promotions, increments, and the release of faculty members. The immediate task confronting the

committee is to establish criteria for appointment, rank, and promotions. The membership of the Committee is composed of the President (ex-officio), the Vice President for Academic Affairs, (non-voting), the Vice President for Financial Affairs (non-voting), and three members elected annually by the Bryant Faculty Federation from the faculty of the college. The faculty representatives for 1967-68 are Louise H. Cronk, Associate Professor of English; Henry L. Foley, Assistant Professor of Accounting; and Earle A. Messer, Associate Professor of Business Administration.

The Curriculum Committee's duties are to review the offerings of various programs in all schools of the college and to

BRYANT STUDENTS STAGE RALLY

SUCCESSFUL SHOWING . . .

James Gibney, President of the Senior Class, along with other student senate members, address the throng of rallying students in front of Dean Gulski's office.

Just a few of the over 800 students who marched around south hall in support of the student senate.

determine the addition, deletion, and revision of courses and degree programs. The Committee's first business shall be to clarify the academic objectives of the college. The Bryant Curriculum Committee is composed of the President (ex-officio), the Vice President for Academic Affairs (non-voting), and four other members elected annually by the Bryant Faculty Federa-

tion from the faculty. Current faculty representatives on this committee are Wallace S. Camper, Instructor in Business Administration; James R. Estey, Instructor in History; Thomas A. Manion, Associate Professor of Economics; and Clarissa H. Patterson, Assistant Professor of English and Secretarial Studies.

Bryant Students have finally awakened to the reality of the world around them. On Wednesday, December 13th, a student-supported Senate rally was held in front of South Hall to present to the administration of this institution certain grievances that had to be aired. The furor on the part of the students was brought to a head the week before when the registrar's office published the new exam schedule for this semester. It happens that the schedule has been tightened up to the point where many students have one exam after another in three day's time.

Among the complaints by students is the cut system here at Bryant. Many feel that, at this point in the school's history, it is time to change—to get in step with other educational institutions.

The problems encountered in taking six courses and in dropping courses, the problems of determining what professors are teaching what courses, the rule that every course must have three tests—causing a student to be taking many exams in a week's time, and the ways that the students found out about our tuition increase and other college developments are among the many reasons which led to Wednesday's rally.

With the coming of Christmas, the rally was appropriately timed. During this season it was hoped that the soft hearts?—of our superiors might be found to derive solutions to these and other problems. Let us hope that 1968 will find Administration—Faculty—Student communication helping to remedy problems and increasing understanding among all the interests at this college.

Students could see that with unionization, the college community had agreed that faculty should share in decision-making power, and they asked whether students, as well, should not have a voice in decisions that affected them. Bryant students had a senate, but this body made decisions about the social calendar and had little influence in other matters. It was not a representative body with power to affect important decisions.

Unmistakable evidence of discontent appeared early in the sixties when students protested the meal plan: they had to buy all three meals daily at the college cafeteria. Students organized a demonstration to demand a modified plan for those students who chose not to eat every meal on campus. Gardner Jacobs agreed and instituted the modifications. The inflexibility of the rules governing academic and social life continued to rankle. Protests in the late sixties began with a challenge to specific rules and ended with a change in the power structure.

On December 13, 1967, eight-hundred students marched around South Hall to demonstrate support for the student senate which had protested the final examination schedule. According to administration rules, every course had to have three examinations a semester and a final examination, no matter what the course or teaching method. This meant that a student taking six courses would have to take that many tests in less than a week. By final examination time when the registrar published the schedule, some students found that they would have to take six final examinations within a three-day period. The student senate asked the administration for student participation in the scheduling of examinations. Students eagerly joined the demonstration to support their senate. They were also reacting to the shock of a sudden increase in tuition imposed on them.[49] Their demands were not met immediately, but the demonstration revealed that the desire for change was building.

The faculty-student relationship was one situation on which students chose to concentrate. The next month, January 1968, the students demanded and obtained a grievance procedure. Seven students, appointed by the president of the student senate from the sophomore, junior, and senior classes, formed the committee. A student could submit a written statement of his or her grievance. The grievance was discussed and a proper course of action agreed on: the recommendation was eventually forwarded to the appropriate administrator and acted upon.

In March, the student senate worked out a systematic way for students to evaluate courses and faculty teaching. The first course and faculty evaluation sheets were handed out and the first evaluation report published on March 8, 1968. It is interesting to note that the students were reluctant to give any faculty member a poor rating and eager to praise in their written comments.[50]

In December 1968, the student senate, responding to students' requests, submitted a new policy governing absences from class. Up to this point, a student was penalized if he or she took more than the allowed two cuts per class. Students demanded unlimited cuts for all those upper classmen who had a grade point average of 3.00 or above.[51] The administration agreed reluctantly. The new system eliminated a lot of record-keeping chores because many professors stopped recording absences in upper level courses.[52]

The student newspaper, *The Archway*, had always had a faculty member appointed by the administration who read all copy and made changes before the paper went to print. During March and April 1968, students working on the paper requested meetings with "the brass" (as they called the top college administrators) to define the limits of the

After the faculty formed a union to gain more power, the students decided that they, too, wanted a voice in decision making.

faculty advisor. During the previous year, news copy had often been rejected with the remark, "You can't criticize the administration!" When the new academic year opened in September 1968, the paper was published without a faculty advisor.[53] In subsequent years, when the staff again had an advisor, there was no censorship.

Also frustrating to the students was the inflexibility of the rules governing their social life. Students were aware that other colleges were dropping such rules as dress codes, curfews, and sign-in and sign-out sheets. It was inevitable that Bryant students would question their own system of rules. Although men's dormitories had no curfews, women's dormitories continued to have curfews of ten o'clock on week nights and midnight on weekends. Spring and fall of 1969 proved to be a time of testing these limits. Some things were not changed—students never gained the right to bring beer or any alcoholic drink into the dormitory. But, students did successfully challenge the rule that no one could bring a friend to his or her room. One May weekend the dormitories had a trial "open house" during which students could bring friends, including members of the opposite sex, to their rooms for parties.[54] Housemothers, faculty, and administrators were impressed by the civility of the occasion, and the rule was altered to permit visitors at stated times. Women's dormitories got a new curfew of 2:00 A.M. on Friday and Saturday and midnight on Sunday, plus four "lates" a semester. However, women still had to sign in and out of dormitories when they went out after 6:00 in the evening.

Dress codes continued to be strict: men had to wear coats and ties in the dining hall, while women had to wear dresses or skirts and blouses, hose, and heels. The Women's Residence Association (a committee of women's dormitory presidents) had a rule that pants could be worn in the dormitory only after three o'clock in the afternoon and the college rule stated that pants could not be worn in the classroom buildings at any time. In the cold autumn of 1969, women students demanded that they be allowed to wear slacks to class and all around campus. Both the dean of men, William Smith, and the dean of women, Philomena Castronovo, favored changing the rule but strictly enforced it as long as it was on the books.[55] The Women's Residence Association changed the rule, and the college followed suit for classroom buildings and the library.[56]

In the midst of these changes, another event took place which profoundly altered power relationships at Bryant. In 1969 Gardner Jacobs took a step he had been contemplating for some time: he relinquished the presidency to become chancellor so that he could devote all his efforts to raising funds for a new campus. Now, Jacobs, the board of trustees, administrators, and faculty sought a distinguished scholar to enhance the college's reputation. The person they found was Schuyler Hoslett. He had been on the faculty of the Graduate School of Business and Public Administration at Cornell University and later taught at Columbia University where he founded and directed the Executive Program in Business Administration. He was a vice president of the Dun and Bradstreet Group. He was also a noted author and had lectured all over the country. Equally important was the fact that he was a warm, approachable person who liked being with students.[57]

When Hoslett became president, the board of trustees changed its demeanor vis-à-vis the college's chief administrator. For the first time since 1916, the college had a president who was not a Jacobs. The elder Jacobs, Harry, had informed the board before he had taken an action and it had been approved; the son, Gardner, had "consulted" before he did whatever he was determined to do. Now the board members discussed

Schuyler Hoslett became the first Bryant president since 1916 who was not a Jacobs.

upcoming decisions and sometimes even voted no. They began to take initiatives in setting policy.

Students perceived that a shift in the power structure had occurred and that the board of trustees now had some power. They demanded student representation on the board. By the beginning of November 1969, the senate had collected over one thousand names on a petition requesting representation.[58] The Board did not grant this request.

In the spring of 1970, the students once more challenged the college administration. On March 6, fifteen hundred students began a demonstration which continued as a protest on the lawn of South Hall for several days. The student senate, responding to student demands, had asked college administrators to change the calendar so students could finish the semester before the Christmas break. They wanted the first semester to begin on September 9 and end on December 21; and the second semester to start on January 26 and end on May 10.[59] Also, they felt their difficulties with the system of registering for classes had to be overcome. One student described the situation: "Registration was long and tedious, and you didn't have a chance to get the courses you wanted or needed."[60] Students asked that a computer be programmed to facilitate registration and that students be able to choose courses, times, and instructors. Finally, they had become aware that minorities were not represented in the administration and faculty, and they wanted minority representation. The front page of The Archway expressed their situation in historical terms: "THE DEMANDS OF THE STUDENTS WILL BE MET. For as in France, we, the Third Estate, are both the majority and the future leaders."[61]

In a mass meeting on March 16 the student body voted for three proposals: changes in the current calendar, changes in registration procedures, and additional black administrators. Three days later, the administration agreed to the proposals, but no timetable was set and the wording of the reply to the student senate was vague. Nevertheless, the student senate appointed a committee to work on each issue.

On March 19, when the next student assembly met in the gym, the feeling most in evidence was determination. When the student government president Lynn Hayden read the administration's reply, students began calling for the administrators to come in and speak to them directly. Vice president for academic affairs, Tom Manion, agreed to address the students. Manion reported progress in working with the student committees on the first two proposals; however, he had to admit it was difficult to recruit black administrators and teachers. They were very much in demand by colleges everywhere because, suddenly, colleges were attempting integration at all levels. Manion asked that the administration and the student committee be given time to work on this.[62]

The result was that the yearly schedule was changed so that the first semester ended before Christmas. An improved system of registration was worked out: seniors registered first, then students with jobs which placed restrictions on their class schedules, then juniors, then sophomores. Freshmen continued to follow schedules prepared for them. Final examinations were reduced to one hour and it was left to the individual professor to decide if finals were appropriate to the course and teaching method. The committee and administration developed a hiring policy and worked desperately to find black scholars willing to come to Bryant.[63] But all over the nation, administrators were finding that years of not welcoming young minority students to colleges—who would have become these leaders—had resulted in a dearth of senior scholars from minority groups.

From December 1967 to the spring of 1970, the students changed their college significantly: the student senate, formerly a body which had debated the social calendar, became both a repository for student concerns and the organizer of mass protests to obtain the reforms students wanted. Lynn Hayden, the student government president in 1969–70, was determined to extend student power by placing students on every college committee dealing with issues that affected the student body.[64] There was student input regarding the academic calendar, teaching evaluations, registration procedures, social regulations, and in the case of minority faculty, even hiring practices.

While the students were reshaping their role in the college, there were developments in the academic program. A graduate school was initiated in September 1969, strongly supported by President Schuyler Hoslett. In the spring of 1970, Sol Lebovitz, the chairman of the social science department, became acting dean of the Graduate School. The new degree that Bryant offered–the Master of Business Administration–was eagerly sought by business men and women in the state who needed a graduate program in the evening.

Lebovitz had come to Bryant College in 1962 from an executive position at the International Office Dictaphone Corporation in New York. A graduate of Boston University, he had taken his master's and doctorate in political science at Harvard.[65] He was relentless in finding qualified people to teach: they had to have a Ph.D., or if they were accountants, a CPA. If they taught taxation, they had to have a law degree; if they taught public administration, they had to be experienced in government work. As often as possible, graduate faculty were drawn from the regular faculty; but Lebovitz also hired experts in the community. In developing the graduate program in business administration at Bryant, he followed the guidelines determined by the American Assembly of Collegiate Schools of Business.[66]

Students were admitted to the Graduate School on the basis of their performance on the Graduate Management Admissions Test, their undergraduate record, and their work history. Sometimes Lebovitz would take a chance on a student who showed high motivation at the time of application even though motivation might have been lacking earlier. Usually if a student could make it through the first semester, he or she could finish the program. Twelve courses were required–two courses per semester for three years. Special efforts were made to recruit women and minorities, but the majority of the students were men. Lebovitz decided to try an experiment: Bryant would offer courses in various parts of the state where the students were clustered. For example, Raytheon Corporation asked Bryant to offer graduate programs for employees at their Middletown plant. Aided by such innovations, the overall graduate program proved to be a great success. In the beginning there were only 71 students; ten years later, there were over 1,300 graduate students.[67]

Although Schuyler Hoslett had given his strong support to the founding of the Graduate School, he sometimes postponed decisions, pleading "new man on the block."[68] It soon became clear that he was ill. He resigned, and at the beginning of 1970, Dean Nelson Gulski became acting president while a committee searched for a new president. Gulski provided the wise and compassionate leadership the college needed during its last year on the East Side and especially during the turbulent spring of 1970.

The year 1969–70 was a time of crisis in the nation, and campuses everywhere felt the repercussions, especially in the spring of that year. Bryant was no exception. The war in Vietnam had stirred the consciences

Nelson Gulski (right) congratulates Richard Smith, a Rhode Island legislative intern. Gulski served as acting president after Hoslett became ill and resigned.

of American citizens; for male students, the draft loomed in their future. The war had been a concern of a group of students on the Bryant College campus for several years. In 1967 a series of programs and debates on the war had brought the issues before the students. For example, in October 1967, the World Affairs Forum presented a debate on United States involvement in Vietnam—Professor James Estey, historian, arguing against and Professor Sol Lebovitz, political scientist, arguing for.[69]

In letters to *The Archway* in 1968, 1969, and 1970, students expressed their sense of horror and outrage over the war, and many students began to wear black armbands as a sign of their concern. Student senate president Lynn Hayden said, "We'd see people dying all the time and thought if it wasn't for me being here in school, I'd be dying, too, probably."[70] She described the anti-war protesters as a "mixed group": some were fraternity men, some were the high academic achievers, some were

The "Dialogue with Diplomats" lecture series during the tenure of Schuyler Hoslett (center) brought State Department officials to campus.

When students arrived on College Hill in 1969, the war in Vietnam was the big issue on campus.

well-informed, others went along because their sweethearts were there. Several times they went down to the center of Providence and joined with Brown and Rhode Island School of Design students in protest demonstrations. Bryant students were in contact with national peace groups, and in October of 1969 they formed the Bryant Chapter of the Vietnam Peace Action Committee. They observed the October 15 moratorium. The next spring, Bryant students voted overwhelmingly for the immediate withdrawal of United States forces in Vietnam.[71]

Then on May 6, 1970, at Kent State University, four students protesting escalation of the war were killed. Bryant students, like students everywhere in the nation, voted to strike to protest the bombing of North Vietnam, American intervention in Cambodia, treatment of political prisoners in Vietnam, and the killing of the four students. Bryant students were the first in the Providence area to make that decision.[72] Lynn Hayden summed up their intention: "Somebody – and as many somebodies as possible – had to say something was wrong!"[73] Students and faculty made the strike a time for learning. "Teach-ins" about the history of Vietnam and the current war went on as well as theatrical and musical presentations of the aspirations of the country's young people for a "truly democratic society." Students set up a telephone network in the gym so that Bryant students could maintain contact with students at other colleges and universities around the country.

Faculty and administrators were generally sensitive to the students' feelings and respectful of their desire to educate themselves on United

PRECEDING PAGE:
Sol Lebovitz was the first dean of the Graduate School, which was established in 1969. He emphasized high standards in admissions and in faculty recruitment.

States foreign policy and the war. They accepted that this was a crisis in the nation's history and gave up on "business as usual." At the end of the semester, those students who wanted to take final examinations took them. Others accepted a grade based on their work up to May 8. The understanding shown the students first by President Hoslett and then by Acting President Gulski set the tone. The Bryant community passed through the crisis with dignity and respect for all individuals involved.

The work of the college went on. Especially notable was a reorganization at the top of the administrative ladder. In April 1970, the college was again submitted to scrutiny by the firm of Knight and Gladieux. The organizational experts recommended that Bryant appoint four vice presidents: academic affairs, business affairs, student affairs, and development and public affairs. The trustees voted to follow the recommendations and chose Frank Delmonico as vice president for business affairs; Thomas Manion for academic affairs; William C. Smith (former dean of men) for student affairs; and Joseph Hagan for public affairs. On June 5, 1970, the board of trustees announced that it had chosen Harry Evarts, a dean at Ohio State University, to be Bryant's next president. Evarts, who had a doctorate in business administration from Harvard, had taught at Northwestern University and Ohio State. He had written a book on business management as well as a number of articles and had acquired a national reputation.

The decade closed with the modern, democratically-run college looking to the future. Gardner Jacobs had become president in 1961; in the nine years since then, the college community had completely transformed itself. From control by a few at the top of the administrative structure, the faculty had moved the college to a system of shared governance. The students had demanded and obtained representa-

tion on committees affecting them and they had changed some of the onerous rules governing social life. A graduate school had been initiated and was already a major concern. Roy Nelson, assistant director of admissions, said he felt lucky to have been there: "Few people can be a part of growth such as this."[74]

In the spring of 1970, the college had a new president, Harry Evarts, as well as four new vice presidents.

FIVE

Bryant College in Smithfield: A New Campus

Earl Tupper was so impressed with Bryant that he decided to donate his Smithfield farm to the college rather than sell it.

The library was given high priority in the design and planning of the new campus.

THE BRYANT COLLEGE community began to feel the need for better classroom facilities, an adequate gym, faculty offices, and a modern library. There were height restrictions on the East Side so the college could not build the tall buildings it needed; and given the lack of space in the crowded residential area, it could not expand horizontally. The twenty-seven buildings spread out on the East Side presented a total heating bill each winter that was enough to discourage the most optimistic of the college's financial officers. Each dormitory–in reality, a large private house–had to have a housemother and a cleaning staff, and these personnel expenses further increased costs. Parking continued to be a nightmare. The joke was that it took five years to get a Bryant College degree: four years in classes and one year hunting for a parking place. In their dreams, administrators saw signs on the familiar buildings saying, "Bryant College Has Moved–Please Apply at the New Campus."

Sites for a new campus were suggested, but each had serious drawbacks. The college–which had no endowment–had very little money in reserve. It existed on tuition income and showed a modest surplus each year.[1] Gardner Jacobs heard from a professor who lived in Smithfield that Earl Tupper, president of the Tupperware Corporation, wanted to sell his 220-acre estate in the town. Tupper expected a price of $75,000 to $100,000, and college officials knew that the Boy Scouts were interested in buying the land. Nevertheless, Jacobs told Frank Delmonico, the vice president for business affairs, to contact Mr. Tupper.[2] Tupper referred Delmonico to his agent. Six months later, Tupper called Jacobs from Providence's Biltmore Hotel and said, "I understand you want to buy my property."[3]

Gardner Jacobs and Gertrude Hochberg went to the Biltmore to meet Mr. Tupper. They carried a college catalog with them and sat and talked about what the college was doing. "You promise to help every student get a job? That's a good college. I like the idea!" Tupper said. He added, "I might give you the land."[4]

Jacobs and Hochberg were so dazed they had trouble finding their car to return to the college. Later, Delmonico and the director of the physical plant, Joseph Murphy, toured the grounds with Tupper and Jacobs. Delmonico immediately spotted the right place for the central building—a rise with a 360° view of the rolling hills and trees of western Rhode Island.[5]

That evening, Jacobs went over to the Biltmore to have dinner with Earl Tupper. The next day, Friday, as Jacobs walked into Tupper's suite at the Biltmore, the telephone rang (it was the college lawyer wanting to talk to Jacobs). "What did you do, hypnotize the guy?" he asked. "He's going to *give* you the property!"[6] Jacobs drove Tupper to the airport so Tupper could take his plane to the Bahamas. On Monday, Tupper returned and signed the papers. Tupper remarked to reporters, "You sort of like to give something to a school like that."[7]

People at Bryant felt that on that day—October 24, 1967—an angel had dropped out of the heavens. The angel did not bring funds to *build* a new campus in Smithfield, however, and Bryant had only about $300,000.[8] A new campus would cost millions. Delmonico dealt with the very cautious board of trustees which rightly asked how a college with no endowment and a relatively small end-of-year income could qualify for millions of dollars in loans. In the late 1960s, Delmonico and the college controller, Frank Albright, raised tuition and cut costs wherever possible. They achieved a net income of $600,000 a year.[8] An aggressive admissions department increased the number of students.

Delmonico, Joseph Hagan, vice president for public affairs, and Gardner Jacobs went to Washington to talk to officials at the Department of Housing and Urban Development (HUD). Hagan had come from Washington and had contacts there, and Gardner Jacobs had also established relationships with people in HUD. Shortly after this initial meeting, negotiations on details were switched to the HUD regional office in Boston. The three talked about Bryant's needs: Jacobs interviewed the

The 220-acre Tupper property included the old Mowry homestead, which was moved to a new site so that the unistructure could command an impressive view.

Frank Delmonico and Thomas Manion (here flanking Nelson Gulski) were two of the new vice presidents appointed in 1970. Delmonico handled the business aspects of building the new campus and selling the old one.

head of the agency; Hagan talked to the planners; and Delmonico sat down with the financial experts. Delmonico said that as they talked, the numbers grew. Finally, they received five million dollars as an outright grant and five million dollars in interest subsidy. This meant that the federal government agreed to pay whatever interest beyond three percent Bryant's building loan would require.[9]

Delmonico then went to the board and said, "Look, we now have five million dollars and we can sell the East Side campus for five million." He persuaded them that, with this amount and with the government picking up the bill for interest over three percent, Bryant College could borrow the remainder of the $17.5 million needed to build a splendid new campus. The trustees agreed and the college issued bonds. They sold within a few days.[10]

Of course, there was only one potential buyer for the East Side campus—Brown University. Delmonico went through photographs and drawings of buildings, selected a representation of each building Bryant owned (with square footage noted), put these in a loose-leaf notebook, and walked over to Brown. Malcolm Stevens, vice president for business affairs at Brown, and Frank Acker, special assistant to Brown's president, took him seriously. "I had never sold anyone any-thing—let alone an entire campus," Delmonico said. They talked. Delmonico promised that Bryant could vacate the East Side campus within three years.[11] Brown officials knew that Bryant was "under the gun." Nevertheless, Brown University expected to expand. And, in fact, increasing enrollment was causing it to look for every available dormitory room and classroom. Brown negotiated with Delmonico building by building.

At the end, attorneys reduced their discussion notes to a contract. In the contract Brown paid five million dollars for twenty-six buildings and 10.9 acres of land; but because part of this sum finished paying Bryant's mortgage on one dormitory building, Bryant received a net of $4.3 million.[12] The formal announcement of the sale was made on March 20, 1969, by the presidents of the two educational institutions.

Delmonico had hoped for more money from the sale. No one had mentioned furniture, so Delmonico went back to Brown and this time he met the people in charge of residence halls. Brown officials bought the furniture for two-hundred and fifty thousand dollars. They were glad to get it because students were expected too soon to order furniture. Fur-thermore, Bryant administrators had no intention of taking beds, chests, and desks with them to Smithfield.[13]

It became clear that the college, with its government grant for interest subsidy, could manage a higher loan than anticipated. It was decided to invest the entire sum from the sale to Brown so that the college would have an endowment.[14] Meanwhile, the college began its first capital fund drive in April 1970.[15]

All through 1968, while college administrators were negotiating the sale of the East Side campus to Brown, they were also looking at building designs.[16] One day Gardner Jacobs received a query letter from a small architectural firm headed by a twenty-eight-year-old named Robert Hillier. The firm, based in New Jersey, had just finished building dormitories for Fairleigh Dickinson University. They were small, low-cost, and efficient. Hillier was writing to colleges all over the northeast asking if they were considering building a new dormitory. Jacobs wrote on the enclosed post card, "We're considering building an entire campus." Immediately, Hillier came up to see Jacobs. After talking to Jacobs, he walked the Tupper land with Vice President Joseph Hagan. "It was spectacular!" Hillier said.[17]

The college administrators and the board of trustees met shortly afterwards to hear architects' plans for the new campus. Most were Rhode Island architects and construction firms which came in with drawings of buildings they had completed and which they were sure board members knew about. Robert Hillier chose instead to study the site and build a gigantic scale model of the terrain and the building he would construct. He left his home in Princeton at five o'clock in the morning, drove through a snowstorm, and arrived at the college that afternoon at four with the scale model.[18] The board was dazzled by his presentation.[19]

Gardner Jacobs sent a delegation to Fairleigh Dickinson University to see the structures Hillier had built there. One person talked to students; another, to faculty; another, to maintenance people. Vice President for Student Affairs William Smith especially liked the dormitories because they were large enough to be efficient, but not so large that the student would be deprived of the feeling that he or she had a comfortable home. Each suite of three bedrooms had a living room.[20]

Architect Robert Hillier shows a model of his innovative design for the unistructure to Gulski and a student, John Horton. Hillier had been awarded the contract to design the campus partly on the strength of the initial model that had accompanied his proposal.

After further research, college administrators and trustees asked
Hillier to come back for another interview in February 1969. They
pressed Hillier to give them an estimate on the time it would take for his
firm to build a new campus. His reply–twenty-six months–settled the
issue. Every other firm had said, "Four years at the least." The next
morning, Hagan called Hillier and told him he had the job. "It was the
biggest moment of my life," Hillier said.[21]

Hillier and a team of seven people from his firm spent months that
winter living in the eighteenth-century farm house on the site, studying
wind direction and velocity, land contours, and the amount of rainfall
and snow. Many days, Hillier walked the land, worked over layouts with
his staff, discussed ideas with Lionel Mercier and Joseph Hagan, and sat on
Frank Delmonico's floor, bent over drawings.[22] A planning committee,
chaired by Lionel Mercier, vice president for academic affairs, worked
with Hillier and his staff. Every constituency in the college community
was represented on the committe–students, faculty, administrators, and
staff, including the head of maintenance and the cafeteria manager.[23]
In addition, Hillier's staff regularly interviewed people at the college.

The initial model had been a campus of several buildings and so
was the next one. But the more the architects surveyed the cold, wind-
swept site, the more they thought, "Wouldn't it be nicer if people would
just make it to one building, take off their coats, and be comfortable?"[24]
They were working within a tight margin–cost per square foot had to
be kept down. When there were many classroom and office buildings,
each had to have a lobby, elevators, men's and women's rest rooms, fire
escapes, etc. With one building, there could be one magnificent lobby
and fewer elevators, fire escapes, and rest rooms. Each model was
presented to the board of trustees. When Hillier showed the board
members and administrators how much less energy loss there would be
with one building instead of several, they were impressed. As each
model was designed, it went out to bid. The unistructure proved to be
the most economical to build, and that clinched the decision.[25]

All drawings and materials were presented to the board. Again,
everything went out to bid, and there were eventually about fifty separate
contracts. Hillier said, "Frank Delmonico made sure we could afford
everything we were doing."[26] The Gilbane Company was awarded the
contract to build the unistructure; Dimeo Construction Company, the
dormitories (one of which included the infirmary); and Donatelli Building Company, the gym. The total cost came to $17,000,000: unistruc-
ture, $7,500,000; dormitories, $5,000,000; gymnasium, $1,300,000;
furnishings and equipment, $950,000; site work and utilities, $700,000.[27]
The total cost per square foot of the new campus was twenty-three
dollars–an astoundingly low sum. A building in the state university
system going up at the same time cost forty-six dollars per square foot.[28]

The library was of special concern. On the old campus, the library
had been moved from place to place and then settled in a large mansion, with additions built later. However, the library had never been
entirely satisfactory. In 1968 the college hired John Hannon as director
of library services. Hannon found holdings of only 35,000 volumes, all
classified according to the Dewey decimal system. He surveyed the
holdings and soon realized that many books had been acquired through
book drives–people had just cleaned out their cellars and given the
books to Bryant. There had been no regular ordering process. He sold
duplicates or traded with other libraries and then reclassified all books in
accordance with the Library of Congress system. Next, he investigated
the possibility of federal grants and was able to obtain a government grant

of $17,000 to purchase needed books, with the promise of additional annual funds.[29]

Hannon was then ready to project the number of holdings Bryant could expect to have during the next fifteen years, and he sat down with Hillier to plan the new library. First of all, he wanted the library to be at the center of the campus, easily accessible to everybody. There was no doubt that it must be in the unistructure. Inside the library, he wanted a traffic pattern that would make it easy for the student to get materials: he insisted that the card catalog be easily spotted so it had to be placed near the entrance. The reference desk and circulation desk had to be near the entrance, as well. Hannon talked to faculty and found they wanted an audio-visual department and an excellent reserve system. He surveyed the student body: they wanted study rooms, smoking lounges, and study carrels. Whenever Hillier asked, "What do you want today, Jack?," Hannon was ready to give the details.[30]

Hannon wanted the library to be inviting and had visions of wood, soft colors, and comfortable furniture. The architects suggested metal furniture; he insisted on wood. When he found that the Jens-Rison factory in Connecticut would make beautiful furniture of wood at a lower cost than metal, the architects agreed to this choice.[31]

Hillier, his associates, and the committee tried to include all the features the college community desired, with as few compromises as possible. Students wanted a swimming pool, for example, and a student union with recreational facilities such as a game room and bowling alleys. The architects found that if the swimming pool were placed in the gymnasium and used for classes it would have to be regulation size, an expensive item in a strained budget. Dean Mercier proposed that they build a pool but put it in the unistructure so that it could be smaller, but more accessible for recreational use by everybody— students, faculty, and staff.[32]

Hillier had designed large offices to be shared by several faculty members; but on the faculty's advice, he redesigned the existing space to

The unistructure was completed on time and within a very tight budget. By combining so many functions in one building, the overall cost was kept well below that of other new college buildings in the state. (Foreground: architect Robert Hillier.)

accommodate private and semi-private offices. The rule was that if a faculty member wanted a window, he or she had to share an office; if privacy was desired above all else, the instructor had to compromise and accept an office without a window.[33] In the finished unistructure, the desired facilities such as a student union, swimming pool, 500-person capacity auditorium, cafeteria, faculty dining hall, bank, post office, bookstore, station for student-operated radio, and library—not to mention administrative and faculty offices and classrooms—were all there.

College administrators realized there was no suitable entrance to the new campus. The only road approaching the site was an old farm road, Mowry Road, picturesque in its windings through the countryside but potentially treacherous as the access route to an entire campus. Frank Delmonico talked to families living on Douglas Pike who owned property adjacent to the new campus. He located one particular piece of property that seemed to be the most desirable and found that the family who owned it wanted to sell. Bryant bought an acre for $5,000 and thereby acquired a spectacular entrance on the Douglas Pike.[34] Even before the building plans were decided on in detail, workmen began preparing the entrance and drive.

At first, some citizens in the town took a dim view of the prospect of having an entire college move in. The town was only twenty-six square miles with a population of 13,292 people. Townspeople were afraid that rowdy students would necessitate an increased police force and, therefore, higher taxes. To try and calm this fear, the Bryant administration sponsored student activities on the Smithfield grounds while the college was still in Providence. Student picnics were held there, and afterwards the students were careful to clean up. The plan worked; the town officials congratulated the students on their manner and tidiness.

Bryant also wanted the town to see that there were advantages to having a college close by. Gertrude Hochberg began planning a fifteen-week course at the college on drug abuse for elementary and high school teachers in Smithfield.[35]

The Smithfield Historical Society was very much concerned that the historic farm on the Bryant College land with its two eighteenth-century houses and barn would be demolished or else modernized beyond recognition. The oldest had been built in 1708 by Captain Joseph Mowry, a descendant of Nathaniel Mowry, one of the first settlers in northern Rhode Island. His home was one of the original colonial homes. For a while, it was "nip and tuck" with the Smithfield town council, as Nelson Gulski remarked. Finally, the college convinced the council that it could preserve the buildings.[36] The college moved the houses and barn to a nearby ridge. A wing that had been added to the main house at a later date was removed, but all three structures were preserved in their original architectural form.

Utilities such as electricity and gas could be brought to the new campus via Douglas Pike. The college brought in two water lines, and townspeople living on either side of the road could tap into town water. Sewage was another issue, however, and a problem not so easily solved. The Smithfield town council announced that it was going to develop the municipal sewage plant. Delmonico made a presentation before the council, offering to pay the town of Smithfield $110,000 (Bryant's estimated cost of building a sewage treatment plant) if a system would be constructed to tie the college in right away. But the town council had to begin development on the other side of town where most of their residents lived. Bryant had to go it alone.[37]

At the site selected for Bryant's sewage treatment plant, construction workers hit rock while digging the long trench. Up until then, the campus had been built without much trouble of that sort, but this trench had to be blasted through the solid rock. The cost of building the sewage treatment plant reached a total bill of $587,000.[38] It was finished just in time: inspection and approval by the authorities came a day before the students arrived. Environmentalists at the college and in town monitored the effluent that poured into the stream and found the water acceptable.[39]

Another snag occurred when the state fire marshal decided every dormitory suite had to have two exits to the corridor. Delmonico, Hagan, and Hillier sat in his office, arguing that the fire code stipulated two exits from every building and that these were provided. They showed him the code's very words—he showed them the section of the code which stated that in the last resort, the fire marshal's demand had to be fulfilled. Hillier redesigned the suites so that a student could go through a door into a narrow passageway that led into the next suite and then into the corridor. The cost overrun was $140,000. The unflappable Nelson Gulski, then acting president, remarked that whenever you build a campus, there's going to be trouble. "I guess this is ours," he said.[40]

Carl Adler, president of the Smithfield town council, Rhode Island governor Frank Licht, and Gardner Jacobs broke ground for the new campus on April 15, 1970.

The groundbreaking ceremony was held April 15, 1970. The construction of the dormitories began in earnest and was completed on schedule by the Dimeo Construction Company. The unistructure, the most complex building, was the last to be finished. The building process was running behind schedule, and Hillier complained to Gilbane Construction Company that they had not put a superintendent on the job who really understood it. Gilbane sent in Albert Libutti. One morning at eight o'clock Hillier met him for the first time. Hillier described that meeting:

I was walking up one of the stairs and this little guy with a hard hat was coming with an entourage of about fifteen people, and he was shouting this and that, giving orders, and he saw me up on the landing. . . . Suddenly he stopped and came to the base of the stairs and said, "Who are *you?*" I replied, "I'm Bob Hillier, the architect." He said, "You (unprintable)! I want to talk to you! Now, you get down here with me. I've got so many questions for you!" We went along and he was asking questions. . . And we were going up this wooden ladder and he stopped halfway up the ladder and he looked at a guy who was sawing and he said, "Now you go remeasure." This is from thirty feet that he looked down and saw a carpenter cutting a piece too long. We went on up, got the problem on the roof and I showed him how to solve it. And we came back down and he said to the carpenter, "Was I right?" And the guy said, "You were right, Al."[41]

At the end of each day, Libutti "walked the job" and whenever Hillier was there, he surveyed the work with him. There were no more delays. A grateful Bryant College conferred on Albert Libutti an honorary bachelor's degree at the next graduation.

In the middle of the summer, the college was notified by the local carpetmaker that the carpet could not be woven by September. Delmonico and Hillier had a weekend to find another carpetmaker: "We

The board of trustees toured the construction site with Hillier. A year and a half after breaking ground, the college moved in.

had to call all the carpet manufacturers we knew, looking for 36,000 square yards of carpeting on a month's notice," Delmonico said. They found a manufacturer who did meet the deadline, but after it was put down, they discovered that the ingredient which prevents static electricity had not been woven in.[42] The carpet had to be chemically treated after it was in place.

On September 1, 1971, Brown was to take over Bryant's old campus. The dormitories on the Smithfield campus were complete but not yet furnished or carpeted. The unistructure's interior was not yet finished. But Bryant had to move. The opening of school was delayed two weeks, and administrators and faculty packed their own boxes of books and files. The move had been planned in detail and everyone worked. Hannon requested a special mover and designed his own moving boxes, each one numbered in sequence and labelled with the correct Library of Congress number and shelf number. In the unistructure, people moved into temporary makeshift offices. On moving day, as Assistant Director of Admissions Roy Nelson stood beside his car which was loaded with all the admissions records, the director, George Craig, remarked, "Don't get lost—we won't know who's coming!"[43]

Craig drove on ahead and started running the vacuum cleaner in the two classrooms slated to become the temporary "admissions suite." People cheerfully adapted to makeshift quarters, unpacking what had to

89

be unpacked, stacking boxes in temporary formation until permanent offices were completed. Hillier observed,

> The sense of purpose and dedication in the administration and faculty was greater than I have ever seen in any school, but the true test was when they moved out here. There was no ventilation, often no lights, and conditions were inhuman. But few complained and somehow they figured that the dream was here, and things would get sorted out.[44]

At the last minute, Frank Delmonico decided that the college needed to take something from the old campus to symbolize the continuity in the college's history. He remembered the wrought-iron grill work at the front entrance to South Hall through which the procession filed on graduation day. The last morning, a rigger met him at seven o'clock in front of South Hall. They loosened the wrought-iron archway and loaded it up. Hillier and Delmonico decided to put it in front of the unistructure, by the pond.[45]

Classes began on September 20, 1971—seventeen months and one day after groundbreaking. Students moved in their luggage and books just as workmen put the finishing touches on the dormitories. Students met the trucks and carried in the last pieces of furniture through the front door, while workmen carried their tools out the back door. Two days before the students came, the dining hall lacked doors, carpet, equipment and lights. It was littered with lumber and broken glass. (Only a cat with her family of kittens lived there, and they later moved to another building.) Within forty-eight hours, it was transformed by construction workers and dining hall staff. The day the students arrived the staff served 2,000 meals in a pristine dining hall.[46] For the next seventy-seven days, while the kitchens were being readied, students ate forty-seven tons of food cooked in Providence and brought to Smithfield by truck.[47]

The experience of being on an entirely new campus was heady. But some students, especially seniors and juniors, missed the old campus. One student said, "I feel that the old campus had more atmosphere and image to it. If you wanted to do something, you could split and go into the city, or you could at least take a stroll down Thayer Street." Another remarked, "On the old campus, the monotony was broken up because every building was in itself a special piece of architecture."[48] Others, especially the freshmen and sophomores, had no attachments to the old location and quickly adapted to the new.

Now that the college was no longer in Providence, and the rural campus was policed by the college's guards, safety was not a problem. Suddenly, there were no more housemothers: they were replaced by resident assistants. There was no more curfew and no more signing-out. Peter Barlow, assistant to the vice president for student affairs, remarked, "A lot of things fell off the truck between Providence and Smithfield."[49] In effect, the move completed the process of liberalizing college rules begun by the students in the last year on the old campus.

Everywhere there was more personal freedom. In the old library, security guards checked belongings when the student left. Now an electronic device did the checking. Librarians had once taken down the names of students who talked. In the new library certain areas were designated "high noise" and discussion was invited. For commuters, the availability of parking space within a short walk to the unistructure took the anxiety out of getting to class. (The college helped students who had formerly depended on the bus to arrange car pools.)

The ornamental metal entranceway to South Hall was brought to the new campus as a souvenir.

As the college became more oriented towards residential students,[50] the administration realized that students had no Thayer Street (a favorite "hang-out" for college students on the East Side). Social and recreational events would have to be provided on campus. A gymnasium, which had been planned for later construction, became an immediate necessity. Hillier had designed the gymnasium, and a grant from HUD was secured for its building. Donatelli Building Company built it at a cost of $1,300,000. Land was cleared for a baseball field, soccer field, six tennis courts, and an all-weather track.

The student population changed. There was no regular public transportation to Providence so students could not seek work off-campus. Although work-study provisions on campus were made, students who applied to Bryant now had to have greater financial support from home. At the same time, applications for admission continued to increase, in part because the modern dormitory, classroom, and library facilities were so attractive. The college became even more selective.

The move was responsible for some changes in faculty relations. In the past only men would sit in "The Hole"; now men and women faculty could sit and talk together in the faculty lounge. Faculty found it easier to arrange appointments with the students now that they had private or semi-private offices. The improved library facilities made class preparation for the instructors and class assignments for students more manageable. But most important of all, people felt they had come out of the "shadow" of Bryant's former neighbor, Brown University. Conscious of the spirit of adventure and beauty the unistructure projected, they saw themselves as a special academic community with a new sense of freedom and confidence in the future.

New traditions have developed around the archway on the Tupper campus. Despite the couple posed here, students do not pass through the arch until they graduate.

The 1970s:
Growth and
Growing Pains

A T THE BEGINNING OF 1971, excitement over the move to a new campus prevailed over difficulties. However, as the decade went on, there were problems brewing, caused partly by astounding growth in enrollment. A new president, Harry Evarts, was assiduous in fund-raising but came to be seen as less attentive to faculty and student needs. Disruptions in college life and the return of a retired dean to be acting president were the most dramatic events. But innovations in programs and the formalization of long-term planning also characterized the decade. By the end of the seventies, the college had another president and a renewed feeling of confidence in the future.

The decade began with a brilliant innovation. Continuing Bryant's tradition of service to the Rhode Island business community, President Harry Evarts decided the college should offer high quality management programs for the professional managers in the state. He envisioned the Center for Management Development and was able to get a $50,000 grant from the Calder Foundation in New York to set it up. Evarts next advertised for an expert in organizational behavior to head the center. After several months of fruitless searching for the right candidate, Evarts appointed his executive assistant, Philip Graf, to be the director and told him to develop the center in such a way that it would enhance the image of Bryant College.[1]

Graf admitted, "I had no experience, only the challenge of a task and a general perception of what needed to be done."[2] But Evarts' hunch that Graf would be creative in the job proved correct. He proceeded to contact "key organizations, top executives, and opinion leaders" who would spread the news about the program and make a commitment to support it.[3] The first year, 1973–74, the center offered eight programs for 157 participants. Some were two-day workshops, some were one- or two-week courses. Among the topics were "Managing and Motivating Employees," "Communications and Managerial Effectiveness," and "The Managing Woman." Graf decided that all workshops had to be set up in response to an identified need and had to have specific educational objectives. He insisted on evaluation of results and established a feedback process so that his staff could reformulate objectives and modify instructional techniques and course design according to participants' needs.[4]

Within five years, the center had established a reputation for quality programs. There were increasing requests for workshops and increasing numbers of participants. In 1976–77, fifty-eight workshops were offered with an enrollment of 1,333. The first year saw a net loss of $35,000 which was covered by the grant. The college picked up the tab for net losses in the next two years, but by 1976–77, the center was showing a surplus of $20,000 and from then on it proved to be financially sound.[5]

At the same time, innovations in the college curriculum itself were being implemented in such areas as computer science and specialized managerial programs. Beginning in the fall of 1971, Bryant announced two new graduate programs: an MBA in accounting and an MBA in management. Wallace Camper suggested a program to prepare students to work in the burgeoning tourist industry – an undergraduate major in hotel management.[6] His suggestion was researched and implemented.

The college had bought its first computer in 1969 when Bryant was still on the East Side. Charles Snyder, a mathematician who had five years of experience working with computers in New York state schools, came to Bryant to be the director of the brand new computer center. At that time, Bryant had its only computer, an IBM 1130 model, housed in a small white building between Memorial Hall and Kilcup Hall.[7] Snyder said, "For the first six months, I sat around interviewing people, trying to figure out what they wanted to do."[8] Although business was slow at first, activity soon picked up briskly. The admissions office entered their data first; then the registrar's office had its records put on computer; several years later, the bursar's records were entered.

Meanwhile, classes where students were learning Fortran and mathematics needed computer time. Next, secretarial students began to use computers. Increasingly, individual professors needed access to the computer to record their research data. It soon became clear that Bryant needed a new and larger system. In 1975, the college bought a Basic Tyme-Share computer and five years later, a Data General. At the end of the decade, besides the three main computers on campus with terminals in administrative offices and two classrooms, there was also a research laboratory equipped with personal computers.[9]

Bryant had a long history of keeping up with changes in office technology and of offering instruction in new machines as soon as need was established. Clarissa Patterson, acting vice president for academic affairs in 1978, convinced the Committee on College Organization to set up a department for instruction in computer use, separate from the management department. The new department – Systems Management – offered a major which became popular with students within a couple of years.[10]

The Graduate School, only two years old at the beginning of the decade, continued to grow despite fears that its location in Smithfield would deter people who would have to commute after a long day at work. Actually, the distance was easily covered in the fifteen-minute drive from Providence (via major highways); and easy parking on the new campus proved to be an attraction for the students. By 1977, the number of graduate students had increased to 780. Admissions standards for the Graduate School were raised. Basic requirements included a bachelor's degree and an acceptable score on the Graduate Management Admission Test or the Graduate Record Examination as well as transcripts showing satisfactory grades in all undergraduate and graduate study.[11]

Generally, the graduate students were working people. A survey conducted in 1976 and 1977 to find out who attended the evening MBA

In 1972, Bryant sponsored a symposium on women in business. Juanita Kreps, James B. Duke professor of economics at Duke University, was the featured speaker and an honorary degree recipient.

program showed that 85 percent were employed, nearly half in manufacturing industries. These students were noticeably older than the undergraduates: two-thirds were in their twenties; nearly one-third were in their thirties; and 8 percent of the graduate students were over forty years old. The great majority (78 percent) chose management as the area of concentration although a sizeable minority (18 percent) chose accounting. About half of the students were reimbursed for tuition by their employers; a little over a quarter received some type of financial assistance from the government.[12] They were serious, job-oriented people who were willing to commit weekday evenings for two years to attend class and study.

Graduate students usually took two courses a semester. Dean Lebovitz wanted to keep the schedule flexible while offering courses at a time and place most convenient to students. In 1979 Bryant started offering graduate courses in the late afternoons and on Saturdays. Also, the college continued to go where students were clustered—such as the Raytheon plant in Middletown. By the end of the decade, proof that Bryant was offering a graduate program that met the area's needs was seen in terms of numbers: Bryant's graduate enrollment was now 1,200.[13]

In the early 1970s, administrators at Bryant College were thinking about ways to encourage women students to come to Bryant. Although the enrollment of women had increased, they were still a minority in the student body. Gertrude Hochberg organized a symposium on women in business to attract the attention of women. Representatives from the development office called on businesses in the area, asking them to pay the costs for young women to attend the day-long event. Letters were sent to every high school within a fifty-mile radius, inviting a counselor and two women students interested in a career in business. Hochberg persuaded Juanita Kreps, at that time James B. Duke Professor of Economics at Duke University, to be the principal speaker. Kreps talked about what it meant for women to be in strategic places in business. Hochberg made sure Bryant and Dr. Kreps received nationwide publicity. Many of the young women who attended the symposium chose Bryant as their college.[14]

As the decade went on, more and more women came to Bryant. No longer did they choose secretarial science courses; now they wanted business administration, business communications, or a specialized program designed to enable them to obtain executive positions. The influence of the women's movement which raised the aspirations of generations of American women was at work. Also, possibilities for advancement were opened up for several reasons: pressure on the government by women's groups forced the enactment of legislation which required fair hiring practices and an end to discrimination in salaries. During the late 1960s and early 1970s, the media publicized the women's movement and spotlighted successful women in business and the professions. Corporations began to consider women in their own ranks for leadership positions and even began to hire women from outside for top jobs. Women, themselves, began to be more assertive in demanding promotions and in seeking executive positions.

In 1863, Ezra Mason had urged women to attend Bryant, Stratton, and Mason's Business College, seeing that the Civil War had brought women into business offices. He optimistically predicted that their abilities would enable them to rise to leadership. It took over a hundred years for his prediction to come true.

Now, expectations were raised among high school women that they could have careers in business. In earlier decades, when admissions officer George Craig had visited high schools and tried to interest women students in an accounting career, guidance counselors had discouraged them, saying, "No one will hire a woman accountant."[15] In the seventies, they spoke differently. The efforts of Bryant's admissions and public relations officers to show that Bryant welcomed women students resulted in increasing numbers of women applicants each year. This was a nation-wide trend: in a survey of ten leading universities, women made up three percent of business students in the sixties; by 1974, they were 19 percent.[16] At Bryant, women students comprised 43.9 percent of the student body by 1977. In 1980, they represented half of the students— 49.6 percent.[17]

In addition to this spectacular increase in the number of women students, there were other changes in the student body. The change in the ratio of residents to commuters (noted earlier as a result of the college's move to Smithfield) can clearly be seen. The attempts to enroll minority students resulted in a small increase, but the numbers were still disappointing. Nine foreign countries and twenty-six states outside of New England were represented in 1977, but the overwhelming majority of students came from the New England states. In fact, 85 percent came from areas within a five-hour drive of the college.[18] By 1980, however, there were forty students from states outside New England and twelve from other countries. College officials took heart in these increases, however small, and continued to hope for a more heterogeneous student population.[19]

The overall number of students grew dramatically at Bryant, and population pressure created problems for the existing facilities. These were the kinds of problems many small colleges wished they had, however, because the early seventies were lean years for the nation's educational institutions: fifty-two of them closed their doors between 1972 and 1974. The National Association of College Admissions Counselors reported that 85 percent of participating colleges and universities had spaces available for the fall of 1972.[20] Bryant College, on the other hand, received applications in increasing numbers. The freshman class in 1974 was the largest in years.

The college became even more selective than it had been in the sixties. By 1979 there were five applicants for every place in the freshman class. Those chosen came from the top quarter of their high school class.[21] This set the standard for the decade that followed.

In the mid 1970s, students requested an improved gymnasium, and women called for the opportunity to play varsity sports.

In 1974, Assistant Director of Admissions Roy Nelson remarked, "The dormitories are not full, they are overflowing."[22] The pressure of the student population had immediate consequences for the college. Nearly all the classrooms in the unistructure were the same size, and faculty soon realized that these classrooms could not comfortably accommodate the fifty-five students or more who crowded in.[23] There was also crowding in the dormitories. In 1974, townhouses were built— modern apartments available only for seniors. (Each building contained both men's apartments and women's apartments.) Although the townhouses provided housing for two hundred and fifty students, the college still needed more dormitory rooms.

The space in the student union section of the unistructure began to be taken up by administrative offices. As the number of students grew, the number of faculty and staff necessary to serve student needs grew. From 1970 to 1980, twenty-five additional professors were hired, bringing the number of faculty to 97; non-faculty personnel increased by twenty-four.[24] Students depended entirely on campus facilities for their recreation and social life and felt the effects of shrinking student union space.

In the 1970s, 90 percent of the resident students were involved in

The 1973–74 men's basketball team garnered a conference championship.

intramural and varsity sports. The 1973–74 basketball team won the Naismith Conference championship, and the varsity bowling, cross-country, and golfing teams won district championships. Bryant teams were highly successful in competition; below this promising surface, however, there were rumbles of discontent. Students wanted better gym facilities and felt it was time for women's varsity athletic teams. The gymnasium, which provided a basketball court, lockers, and a few small equipment and exercise rooms, was not large enough, given the high level of participation. Furthermore, women were excluded by tradition from varsity sports. According to the federal government's Education Act of 1972, women were to be provided with access to all athletic opportunities. The impact of this legislation was first felt in the mid-seventies.[25]

From all these discontents, kindling for a fire was accumulating. The spark came in 1975. To understand the confrontations of that year, some background should be considered. One aspect of the controversy was the president's administrative style. Harry Evarts was an imaginative administrator. He decided to explore the possibility of building a law school for Bryant College in downtown Providence. He proceeded to put in place the Center for Management Development. However, in these ventures, he did not attempt to inform the faculty which wanted to be involved in all phases of the college's development.[26]

Evarts did not always follow the structure for decision-making worked out in the late 1960s. He declined to grant tenure to a faculty member recommended by a faculty committee, and he fired an administrator who had served the college for seventeen years.[27]

Over time, President Evarts seemed to become more inaccessible to students and faculty. When students complained about rising costs, he told them decisions made in the president's office were not their business.[28]

In the 1970s, Bryant began to make a conscious effort to recruit a more diverse student body. For the first time, women were not noticeably outnumbered in the business administration courses.

A critical point came when Evarts suspended security chief William Robbie, who had reported an alleged incident involving Evarts. One result of this event was that the three vice presidents, Delmonico, Hagan, and Manion, threatened to resign.

At the end of January 1973, the student senate discussed the possibility of a student strike in support of the vice presidents, pointing to the loss of Delmonico, Hagan, and Manion as "detrimental to the student welfare and the entire college community."[29] Nevertheless, the board of trustees, aware of the work that President Evarts had done to raise money for the college, reluctantly chose to accept the resignation of the three vice presidents, rather than take action against the president.[30] Evarts continued to head Bryant College for two more years.

Meanwhile, the work of the college went on. Against the advice of a faculty committee, Evarts hired Lowell Smith to be vice president for academic affairs (replacing Tom Manion who had resigned during the controversy).[31] When Smith came to Bryant, he did not know that he was not endorsed by the faculty.[32] He proceeded to demand superior credentials for incoming faculty; however, he sometimes challenged long-standing rules the faculty union had defined. His determination to upgrade the graduate faculty was seen as a positive attribute by many faculty members, but some were displeased by the manner in which he seemed to bypass established procedures.

No one could deny that this was a period when the college acquired some outstanding young faculty. Smith, an expert on monopoly and antitrust cases, had an undergraduate degree from Kent State, a master's degree from George Washington University, and a Ph.D. in industrial relations from the University of Alabama. He had been dean of the College of Business Administration at Loyola University in New Orleans. At Bryant he was determined to build up the graduate faculty and especially to staff the Graduate School with full-time faculty rather than part-time instructors. He initiated a system whereby full-time faculty would teach in the Graduate School; this meant that incoming faculty had to have credentials such as the Ph.D. and publications in their field of expertise. They were contracted for nine hours undergraduate teaching and three hours of graduate instruction per semester. Fortunately, the faculty search came at a time when many of the nation's colleges were in a period of retrenchment and were not hiring. Bryant was expanding and found an abundance of distinguished applicants to choose from. Smith and the dean of the undergraduate faculty, Clarissa Patterson, recruited at professional meetings and at prestigious universities.

Jan Smith, an accounting professor at the college.

Affirmative action was at the heart of the recruiting process. In 1971, the first year department heads convened as a formal group, their purpose was to hear a government representative explain how affirmative action worked. The Council of Department Chairmen wrote a list of guidelines for Bryant to follow. Annually, each chair would submit a report to the Council, describing the department's hiring procedures for that year. The chair had to show that women and members of minority groups were sought and give reasons why a woman or minority candidate was not hired. A composite account based on the department reports was then forwarded to the appropriate government agency.[33]

Patterson, as dean of the undergraduate faculty, was the first woman to become a college-wide administrator. Committed to affirmative action, she and Vice President Smith worked to bring qualified women teachers to Bryant. In 1977, Bryant had twenty-two women faculty members and sixty-five male faculty members. Four years later, there were twenty-nine women and sixty-five men on the faculty.[34] In spite of all their efforts, the departments were not able to recruit black, Hispanic, or Native American scholars.

The positive results of hard work by faculty and administrators did not completely allay the discontent within the college community. In February 1975, maintenance workers at the college went on strike after negotiations for a new contract failed. Faculty members had to decide whether they would honor the picket line maintenance workers had set up. President Evarts and Vice President Lowell Smith sent a telegram to all faculty members, threatening them with dismissal if they honored the picket line. This appeared to be a violation of faculty rights, according to the faculty union's contract. Immediately hand-lettered signs appeared, announcing faculty federation and student meetings.[35]

Students and faculty crowded into the auditorium and voted to begin a boycott of classes on March 4, 1975. The rotunda in the unistructure became the daily site of mass meetings in which grievances surfaced. Students and faculty formulated four demands: the dismissal of Evarts and Smith, a fair settlement for maintenance workers, no retaliation against either faculty members or students who supported the maintenance strike, the faculty boycott, or the student strike, and the formation of a committee to revise the college budget.[36]

Clarissa Patterson, dean of undergraduate faculty, worked to recruit women and minority faculty members.

In addition, students demanded that the college "open the books." They wanted an investigation of allegations that there was a conflict of interest regarding Bryant's food services, legal services, and banking services. They were also concerned about the $225,000 cost of the proposed new house for the president. The students demanded a "more professional resident staff" which could provide a "stronger counseling base." They protested the closing of the unistructure and gymnasium at eleven o'clock and ten o'clock, respectively, on a campus where no other recreational facilities were available. They pointed out that there was no space for large gatherings. And they demanded an expansion of the athletic program to include varsity sports for women.[37]

This time trustees went to the protest meetings.[38] Chairman of the Board Clarence Gifford said the faculty protests and boycott of classes were the "final straw" which convinced the board that the college could not go on with Evarts.[39] Evarts resigned.

Harry Evarts reflected on his last years at Bryant with *Providence Journal* reporters, saying that he had learned the old adage was true: "A college president cannot afford to have two constituencies against him at one time." He added, "That's what I succeeded in doing, getting two angry at me." He admitted that he had misjudged the temper of the faculty and was deaf to the "frustration" of the students.

A trustee investigating committee recommended the formulation of an investment policy, a review of all existing college contracts, and competitive bidding on all new contracts. It recognized the need for a new student union and announced plans to build one.[40] Recognizing the identification of Evarts and Smith in people's minds, the trustees gave Lowell Smith a one-year contract.

Once again, the board turned to Nelson Gulski and asked him to come back from retirement to be acting president. Gulski immediately appointed a committee of five students, three faculty members, and two administrators to plan the new student union. He announced that the Rathskeller (a college tavern) would be renovated for use as a counseling center when the new student union was completed. Women's sports were expanded to include varsity volleyball, softball, tennis, and basketball.

Under Gulski's leadership, the college was able to wind up the spring semester of 1975 and plan for a new year. Gulski successfully steered the college through a year of negotiations on the new student center and uncertainty about the search for a new president. Because he was respected and liked by faculty and students, he proved to be just the leader the college community needed in a most difficult year.

In retrospect, it can be seen that the controversy surrounding the last few years of President Evarts' administration had both negative and positive effects. Board member William Haas said that the college's relationship with businesses remained unaffected. However, internal relationships—between faculty, students, and administrators— suffered.[41] The lack of trust remained as a legacy for Evarts' successor to confront. On the other hand, grievances had been aired and dealt with: the crisis provided the impetus to build a new student union, to offer better counseling services, and to extend opportunities in sports. It was now clear that, at Bryant, administrators had to honor their contract with faculty. Also evident was the role the board of trustees would play as the final arbiter in disputes within the Bryant community. There was no question that the board emerged as a much more potent force at the college.[42]

The counseling center, with additional staff, was set up in 1979. Other student services increased as well. On the old campus, there had been housemothers, students in charge on each floor of a dormitory, a dean of men, and a dean of women. On the new campus, there were two resident assistants in each of the thirteen dormitories and a part-time director of residence life. By the end of the decade, there were thirty-eight resident assistants, one full-time director, one assistant director, an area director, and a resident director for the large new freshman dormitory. Health services also expanded its staff. Rapid growth of personnel in student services was a trend which would be continued into the eighties.

The late 1960s and early 1970s were years of rapid social change on college campuses all over the nation. A sexual revolution was taking place in colleges and universities. Peter Barlow, director of residence life from 1975 to 1985, believed that Bryant lagged behind, that changes in sexual mores were not observed at Bryant until the mid-seventies. Marijuana use, widespread in the 1960s on college campuses, came to the attention of administrators at Bryant in the years between 1968 and 1972. Instances of alcohol abuse were observed throughout both decades. Occasionally a serious incident of drug abuse came to the attention of college officials who immediately reported this to the police. But for the great majority of students, neither drugs nor alcohol constituted a problem.[43]

Bryant, like most colleges and universities in the nation, saw the development of an individual's judgment as one aspect of its mission to educate. In earlier decades, deans and housemothers had enforced curfews and other rules. Now the strategy was not to police, but to give assistance and support to students who were trying to cope successfully with the problems of a new generation.

The board of trustees, emerging from the Evarts era with enhanced decision-making power, had planned to spend up to $1.9 million in building the new student center. The board understood the needs students had expressed; however, financial straits soon forced it to reduce the size of the building and lower costs to $850,000.[44] The building was finished in October 1976 and was named the Koffler Center to honor a generous patron, Sol Koffler, founder of American Tourister.

It was with much enthusiasm and optimism that the college community welcomed its new president, William T. O'Hara, in the summer of 1976. He was a graduate of Trinity College and had taken law degrees at Georgetown and New York University. He had been a practicing

The Koffler Center (opposite) was built as a student union in 1976 but was transformed into a unique computer resource center for students, faculty and regional businesses in 1987. From Salmanson dining hall (below), one can see the Koffler Center through a wall of glass.

William O'Hara was introduced to the Bryant community at the 1976 commencement. Malcolm Forbes, publisher of Forbes magazine, (far left) received an honorary degree. (Left to right are Forbes; Federal Reserve Chairman Arthur Burns; William O'Hara; Nelson Gulski; William Heisler, chairman of the board of Citizens Bank; Sr. Lucille McKillop, RSM, president of Salve Regina College; and David Gardam, vice president of RCA.)

attorney, a public defender, and counsel to a congressional committee. He had taught law at the University of Connecticut Law School and, just before coming to Bryant, had been president of Mount Saint Mary College in Newburgh, New York.

The first three years at Bryant were the most challenging of his life, President O'Hara said, because of the general climate of mistrust which events of the early seventies had created.[45] He immediately declared an "open-door policy" and invited both faculty and students to come in to talk to him. Students found his manner "low-key" and "easygoing" and described him as a "good listener." O'Hara remarked, "If the students weren't here, there would be no reason for us to be here." He added, "People years ago were less demanding, less conscious of their rights in education. But things are better in the long run if people have high expectations of education."[46] O'Hara had worked with the faculty committee system when he taught law and was comfortable with it. Interested in mediation and labor law, he was accepting of unions and of the process of negotiation. The faculty felt that he was a man they could work with.

When William O'Hara came to Bryant in 1976, the college was in need of a president who would listen. His open-door policy was welcomed by faculty and students.

When President O'Hara came, people soon realized he was bent on planning, on setting up a dynamic program that would carry the college into the twenty-first century. Immediately he set up a long-range planning committee. Earlier, the trustees had hired the consulting firm Knight and Gladieux to assist in long-range planning. Now O'Hara formalized planning by setting up a committee whose sole interest was in long-term planning, and he involved the college community — faculty, students, and staff — in this process. During its first phase (the end of 1976 to the beginning of 1978), the committee developed a "statement of philosophy" and identified major strengths and weaknesses in college programs. During the second phase, 1978–79, attention was concentrated on developing goals and objectives and establishing a continuing long-range planning process.

Professor Clarissa Patterson chaired the Long-Range Planning Committee and among the members were administrators, teachers, one student, and President

O'Hara. One of their first recommendations was that the college hire a director of institutional research who would monitor trends, environmental changes, and other factors that affect planning. In response to that suggestion, O'Hara invited a recent graduate of the Harvard Graduate School of Education, Jo-Anne Lema, to be director. In defining the mission of the college, the committee affirmed that the basic thrust had to be excellence in selected areas rather than adequacy in many. All programs had to reflect a commitment to education for business and public service. The committee reiterated that the liberal education component was critical to the student's success and had to be an integral part of every program. It affirmed that the primary responsibility of faculty was teaching. Furthermore, it urged the college to seek an even stronger relationship with the business community and with not-for-profit sectors.[47]

In addition to defining Bryant's mission and stating long-range goals, the committee suggested specific practical objectives, such as maintenance of an enrollment level of 2,600 to 2,700 full-time students; 1,720 of these would be residents on campus. Specific ways to achieve goals were suggested. For example, Bryant would secure the interest of high school students by expanding the recruitment area.

Having set the process of planning in motion, O'Hara turned his attention to the board of trustees. He and board chairman Karl Ericson increased the membership of the board from twenty-one to thirty-six to obtain a greater age range and a wider range of expertise. They limited members' terms so that the college could benefit from the enthusiasm of new members. O'Hara and Ericson organized additional trustee committees and encouraged the placement of students, faculty, and alumni on these committees so that a regular means of communication between the board and the college community could be facilitated.[48] The result of these changes was a better informed and more efficient board.

Sensitive to town-gown relationships, O'Hara conferred with the town council when the college intended to do something that would affect local residents. The college also instituted six scholarships for graduates of Smithfield High School. Some friction had occurred before O'Hara arrived, however. Attorneys for the Town of Smithfield had charged that campus shops violated zoning laws. The attorneys for the college answered that the zoning board had approved plans for a "complete college campus" in 1969. The town's businessmen were vexed that there was a book store, bank, sandwich shop, pub, and gift shop that would be making money but not paying taxes. The college's attorneys assured the town that these were services necessary for students in a rural area lacking an easily accessible shopping district. In 1975 seven students set up BRYCOL, a non-profit, student-run organization, which operated these small shops. Students learned to manage a business and relieved the college of the burden. The zoning board gave the college's student-run organization permission to operate shops, and this successful arrangement continued into the eighties.[49]

By the end of the seventies, the town became favorably disposed toward the college, although it still chafed under what it considered increased expenses for fire and police protection. One point of contention was resolved when, in 1977, at the town's insistence, Bryant tied into the municipal sewage system at a cost to the college of $1,575,000, to be paid over a twenty-year period.[50] Townspeople were glad that the college hired off-duty police officers and firefighters for special events on the campus. Local suppliers were pleased that Bryant purchased lumber and other building materials. Local merchants and restaurant

By the end of the 1970s, the townhouse dormitories, built in 1974, had become a coveted "privilege" for seniors.

Class Day in 1973 was held in the unistructure rotunda, under the dome. Later in the decade, large-scale events were normally planned for the gymnasium or for Janikies auditorium.

owners appreciated the students' business. And invitations to free cultural and athletic events at the college brought townspeople onto the campus.

At the end of the decade Bryant was once more contemplating expansion. Dormitory space was desperately needed as well as a new and more extensive student union. The debt from the 1970 construction of the new campus was being financed at a high rate over thirty years. Luckily, the college was able to refinance the debt. The college could then assume a larger loan to pay for a new dormitory. The Rhode Island Health and Education Building Corporation negotiated the sale of $12,080,000 in higher education facilities bonds and $1,665,000 in special obligation bonds. The dormitory was completed in 1979.[51]

Bryant was not experienced in raising huge amounts of money to pay for a building program. It had been a proprietary institution for so many years that a tradition of alumni support for institutional development had had little time to blossom. Even after becoming a non-profit college, it remained a tuition-based enterprise with no endowment at all until the late sixties when Frank Delmonico set up an endowment with funds from the sale of the old campus to Brown University. Nevertheless, Bryant College alumni had given money to scholarship funds over the years. In the mid-seventies, 100 alumni contributed $26,000 for scholarships at their alma mater.

The first director of development, Joseph Welch, appointed in the late sixties, prepared for an annual fund drive to be kicked off each year at the Alumni Banquet. In 1968, the first Corporations Campaign goal was set at $50,000 and met. Dick Twomey succeeded Welch, serving as director of development in 1974 and 1975.

In 1976, the administration, at Gertrude Hochberg's urging, hired Frazier Lang to direct fund-raising activities. Lang had an undergraduate degree from Brown and a master's from Rutgers. He had been associate director of the Education Funding Research Council for Public Affairs Consultants and just before coming to Bryant, assistant director of development at Brown. The objective during Lang's first year at Bryant was to raise money to build the new student center.[52] He set a goal of $50,000 for the Annual Fund (twice the amount raised previously) and to the surprise of the college community, the goal was achieved. The next year, the Annual Fund totalled $104,000. The third year, Nelson Gulski was named chairman of the Annual Fund, and he threw himself into the task with his characteristic energy. He wrote a widely distributed brochure about Bryant and talked to groups constantly. His theme: "Bryant is a good school—it can be great." Trustees Walter Tillinghast, Karl Ericson, and Jack Renza spent hours contacting donors. With this expert help and the generosity of Bryant supporters, the development office more than met its goal for the Annual Fund by raising $156,000. The amount of all contributions totalled $608,000, boosted by Dr. Percy Hodgson's gift of $250,000 for the Edith M. Hodgson Memorial Library.[53] The next year, 1979, faculty, members of the board of trustees, alumni, and students worked on the fund-raising campaign. The total raised for the Annual Fund was $188,000; contributors numbered 3,300.[54] This achievement won for Bryant the Council for the Advancement of Education—U.S. Steel Award for alumni support. The money went into the college's endowed scholarship fund. The development office, in a very short time, had communicated an understanding of Bryant's special mission and had secured support and good will from alumni and friends.

Thus, by the end of the seventies, Bryant had a new appreciation of the need for support from the wider college community and a new development office, which was proving its value to the college. Bryant had survived an administrative upheaval, confronted its problems, and gone on to solve them. Buildings and services were being expanded to meet student needs. Under President O'Hara's leadership, the college community formalized its long-range planning process and confidently faced the future.

OVERLEAF:
With its facade of reflective glass, the unistructure gracefully unites grass and sky.

SEVEN

The 1980s: The Pursuit of Excellence

I N THE 1980s, members of the college community peered into the twenty-first century and examined the paths they would choose to get there. Expansion continued: a new student union, a multipurpose building, and dormitories were all under construction in the first few years of the decade. There were innovations in academic programs. Especially notable was the strong emphasis on the humanities. New and creative services for students were devised and implemented. Dash, vigor, and spirit infused activity on campus in this optimistic era.

The Long-Range Planning Committee, chaired at the beginning of the eighties by Professor Wallace Wood, defined the college's mission and provided specific objectives for Bryant.[1] Now President O'Hara looked for a way to encourage a daring and imaginative approach to shaping the college for the next century. In 1983, President O'Hara, Chairman of the Board Karl Ericson, and the board of trustees established a strategic planning committee. They charged committee members to think boldly about the future, to let their imaginations run free. The committee members were to disregard costs: the trustees would debate their recommendations and consider costs. The committee was to be concerned with the question, "What do you want Bryant College to be like in the future?"[2]

The Strategic Planning Committee was composed of three vice presidents, Leslie LaFond, Alton Mott, George Petrello, and five members of the faculty and staff, Clarissa Patterson, William Haas, Hsi Li, Robert Behling, and Jo-Anne Lema. They immediately appointed an advisory council to work with them so that they could tap the ideas of a variety of college constituencies. The council included students, administrators of special services, and the president of the faculty union, thereby providing a community-wide base in this process of planning for the future.

The committee worked for over a year and presented its first report to the trustees in September 1984–*Catalyst for Quality*. The report was aptly named, for it was evident that committee members wanted a high quality educational experience above all other goals. Their definition of quality was stringent–nothing less than excellence was expected in the learning environment. The means to achieve this ideal were described in detailed plans. First, committee members turned their attention to excel-

The procession through the archway became a regular part of commencement on the Tupper Campus.

lence in teaching. They advised the college to focus special attention on excellent teaching by establishing distinguished professorships: two endowed chairs in business and one in the liberal arts. The board accepted this recommendation, and trustee Norman Sarkisian '53 played a leadership role by contributiong the largest gift in the history of Bryant College. He established the first chair for a distinguished faculty member, to be called the Sarkisian Chair of Business Economics. The committee also recommended setting up an institute for faculty development to help instructors perfect their teaching skills. Committee members wanted this service to include a teaching laboratory which would assist individuals in the examination of their teaching methods by using video and graphics technology. The recommendation was implemented as the Institute for Instructional Development. Faculty internships, which would get teachers more directly involved with industry, were also envisioned. The committee recommended that chairs of each discipline (referred to as "Educational Managers") would be given release time to construct new curricula in light of students' expressed needs, as well as special funds to finance new projects in teaching that faculty members wished to undertake.[3] This last recommendation awaited faculty discussion and acceptance.

Pat Norton was named the first holder of an endowed professorship at Bryant: the Sarkisian Chair of Business Economics.

Next, the committee members considered ways to develop the undergraduate program. They decided that freshmen could benefit from a required shared learning experience which would be interdisciplinary in nature. Upperclassmen, they felt, should obtain "hands-on" experience by working in industry and non-profit institutions as interns; this would necessitate a further strengthening of the college's internship program. Seniors would have a "senior challenge"– an opportunity to tie together knowledge and skills learned in their four years at college.

To maintain quality in the incoming classes, the committee recommended that Presidential Scholarships (of $1,000 each) be increased from ten to twenty-five. It also recommended that financial aid be continuously increased until 1989. (In 1984, about 11 percent of Bryant's tuition income–a sizeable chunk–was invested in financial aid for students.) The committee warned that Bryant's admissions standards should not be lowered, even if that meant allowing enrollment in the day session to drop from 3,000 to as low as 2,700. They recommended that the Evening Division enrollment remain at 2,000 students, its level in 1984.

A new dormitory was called for, a 300-bed facility which would enable the college to increase its resident population to 2,000 for the first time. The committee pointed out that Bryant's dormitory facilities offered a range of living styles, but there was no central location on campus that could be a "living room." They recommended construction of a center which would serve as the student union and a home for all of the members of Bryant's community. Both the recommendations–for dormitory space and for a student union–were accepted by the board.

The future of the Graduate School also came to the committee's attention, and it recommended that Bryant establish a graduate center, recruit a cadre of full-time graduate students, and offer a doctoral degree in business administration. This would mean that both full- and part-time graduate students would be involved in the college. Their research and that of the graduate faculty would be published and enhance the national reputation of the college. The committee projected a graduate student enrollment of 1,000. While the board approved the development of the master's degree curriculum, the trustees shied away from so ambitious a project as a doctoral program.

The committee considered the question of whether Bryant College should pursue accreditation by the American Assembly of Collegiate

Schools of Business. Committee members were willing to reorganize the curriculum to achieve a higher-quality undergraduate education; but as they studied the requirements of the AACSB, doubts arose about this approach to learning. At Bryant, "parallel programming" was followed: throughout their college experience, students took both liberal arts and business courses. A practical advantage to this system was that the student could assess a variety of business courses in the first two years and could change a major easily during that period. The AACSB's system required more liberal arts courses and they had to be taken during the first two years. Professional courses were clustered in the last two years.[4] Another consideration was that the evening program might be jeopardized by the reorganization of the curriculum demanded by the AACSB. Also, the evening program depended to some extent on part-time faculty, and it was feared that the program would not be able to meet the AACSB standard for staffing by full-time faculty.[5] After much discussion, the committee advised the board not to seek AACSB accreditation.

The trustees were troubled by this advice from the committee. The AACSB was a powerful organization. It had been founded in 1916 to promote the exchange of information among business schools and to improve standards in business education. By 1925 the organization had established minimum conditions for membership. In 1958 the United States Office of Education recognized the AACSB as the accrediting agency for the entire nation in the field of business education.[6] Certainly, accreditation by the AACSB would enhance Bryant's position vis-à-vis its competitors.

Bryant College, on the other hand, had just received a ten-year accreditation from the New England Association of Schools and Colleges. Wouldn't this regional accreditation be enough?, the trustees asked themselves. They looked at Bryant's major competition: Babson College already had accreditation by the AACSB and Bentley College had decided to reorganize its curriculum in order to gain accreditation. Already, a few corporations were asking whether a potential employee was coming from an institution accredited by the AACSB. The board reluctantly came to the conclusion that Bryant would have to obtain this accreditation in order to attract the best students and to place its graduates in the most desirable jobs. They reasoned that at some point in the future, Bryant would face the inevitable and reorganize to meet AACSB requirements.[7]

Strategic planning would continue in the 1980s with additional reports: *Designs for Quality* (1985), *The Quality Difference* (1986), and *Strategies for Academic Quality* (1987). The emphasis in each of these documents was on excellence in educational programs, personnel, and facilities.

In the immediate situation, administrators had to make some hard decisions. One concerned the secretarial department. Typing, shorthand, business communications, office management, and business arithmetic had been the core of its program since the early twentieth century, and over the decades Bryant graduates had maintained a reputation for being excellent secretaries. The viability of this department was important because the teacher education department, which trained teachers to staff the business courses in high schools throughout the state, was closely

The most important technological change in the 1970s was the increased use of the computer. By the 1980s, "bits" and "bytes" were integrated throughout the curriculum.

linked to it. Both programs were outstanding in their fields. Indeed, the teacher education department had enjoyed accreditation by the National Council of Accreditation for Teacher Education since the 1960s.

The secretarial studies department, with its two-year associate degree, had always kept abreast of current developments in office technology. However, by the 1970s, the most important technological change was the increase in computer use and the promise of a paper-free office in the future. The department's faculty asked for word processors so that they could update their program and remain leaders in the field. Administrators realized this would be a costly process—one which necessitated serious thinking about the need for such a program.

There were two problems. First, a two-year program in secretarial skills did not fit the concept of education that administrators and faculty at Bryant now held. Second, enrollment in secretarial courses was dropping. In 1967 the number of students enrolled full-time in the day program for an associate's degree was 336.[8] In 1981–82, there were 235 applicants.[9] Historical developments of the seventies, especially the women's movement, had had their impact on career choice. Women who might have worked for a degree in secretarial studies in an earlier decade now chose business administration or accounting as a major and aspired, not to secretarial work, but to ownership and management. Wallace Wood, mathematics professor and vice president for academic affairs from 1978 to 1983, reviewed the research on high school students' aspirations. He found that the number indicating an interest in studying secretarial work when they reached college was diminishing.[10] The prognosis for the future of Bryant's two-year program was poor.

In the fall of 1981, the college administration decided to phase out the department of secretarial studies. It chose not to spend money to purchase word processors and other equipment necessary to continue that program. Instead, large sums were committed to building up the curriculum in computer usage. Phasing out secretarial studies had implications for the teacher education program which had to be put on "hold," awaiting a future reassessment of need for it.

This sudden dissolution of the secretarial program was an extremely traumatic experience for faculty members long associated with it. A few were ready to retire, but others were not. Two people were placed in other departments; three were asked to get advanced degrees in other subjects and were supported by sabbatical leaves and fellowships. For the remaining professors, their years of service determined their severance pay. The decision left some feeling bitter—either toward the administration for ending the program or toward the union for not protecting them.[11] Faculty outside the secretarial studies department were divided. Some believed that secretarial work in the future would constitute a booming job market for the college-educated person and that Bryant should have committed resources to equipping the department to teach computer skills.[12] Others believed the college had taken a necessary step in eliminating a skills program not consonant with the mission of Bryant College in the eighties and beyond.

An easier decision concerning curriculum was also taken at this time. The college administration and faculty chose to expand the offerings in the humanities. In the sixties, some liberal arts courses had been added; in 1970, Vice President Tom Manion had pared down credit hours in the majors to allow students more time for liberal arts electives. By the eighties, both professors and administrators viewed the contemporary business world as a place where men and women with a knowledge and appreciation of their culture as well as training in business could make the most worthwhile contributions. They also saw that the college graduate needed more than the traditional business courses to lead a satisfying family and community life in the complex world of the late twentieth century. Stanley Kozikowski, a professor of English literature, formulated the general plan to integrate new liberal arts courses into the curriculum. He described this new way of thinking among faculty: "It's no longer enough to simply mind your own business, and a new direction in curriculum at Bryant College is breaking up an age-old tendency in higher education to separate and divide areas of instruction from one another."[13]

This was an important new direction for the college to take: in the past, liberal arts courses had been added in order to comply with requirements for accreditation. Now, faculty whole-heartedly committed themselves to according liberal arts courses equal importance and "equal time." No longer were the liberal arts something a Bryant undergraduate studied once in a while, on the side.

In the next stage of this planning, the administration appointed a humanities coordinator, William Haas, a former trustee who held a doctorate from the University of Fribourg in Switzerland, to discover the liberal arts areas that needed development. He planned "organized dialogue" with students in seminars and forums to find out what questions they were asking about values and the business world, their society, their historical moment, and their interpersonal relationships. He then concentrated on devising ways in which existing courses could integrate topics relevant to their questions. New courses appealing to students' imaginations were also planned.

Professional education was not forgotten, however. The Graduate School began a new degree program in 1980—the first master's of business administration in health care management in Rhode Island. The new dean of the Graduate School, George de Tarnowsky, and a faculty member, Professor Edwin W. Chaffee, designed the courses to provide people working in the health care field with advanced managerial training.[14] The program answered a need in the state and grew each year: there were sixty-one students in 1980 and eighty-seven in 1981.[15]

The college began to offer a post-master's Certificate of Advanced Graduate Studies in 1982. This program was designed to meet the needs of executives in business, government, and non-profit organizations who already had a graduate degree and who sought intensive study in a specific subject pertinent to their jobs. In the field of accounting, for example, an individual might choose the required five courses from a number of concentrations, including "Controllership," "Advanced Accounting Theory and Practice," "Advanced Income Tax Problems," "Accounting for Non-Profit Activities," and "Accounting Information Systems."[16]

Once again, the college considered establishing a law school: the Strategic Planning Committee discussed this possibility. However, a five-month feasibility study begun at the end of 1984 revealed that there were enormous costs involved in setting up a law school—seven to ten million dollars. At the same time, the committee found that law school enrollments all over the nation were declining. The committee advised against the proposal, and college administrators decided once and for all to lay the ghost of the proposed Bryant College law school to rest.[17]

The Strategic Planning Committee had recommended development of the internship program. This effort to give students practical experience in business and to strengthen the college's connections with the business community represented a continuing thread in Bryant's history. The committee recognized that there were practical advantages: the student would gain a credential that would be important when he or she applied for a job upon graduation, and the college internship program would make Bryant attractive to incoming students. Prior to this, a student who wanted an internship experience had applied to the department head who had then arranged an internship for the individual. Reports from these early internships were positive, and so college administrators were favorably disposed towards setting up a program.[18]

In 1980, Hinda Pollard, a professor of management, became coordinator of the new program. She talked to students interested in an internship, reviewed their academic records, and chose sixty juniors and seniors to be the first interns. Pollard called managers and persuaded them to take on the student interns who wanted work experience in their firms. She screened the jobs offered and ruled out any position that did not provide significant work related to the student's major. The reputation of Bryant College and the students' records were so positive that soon Pollard began to receive requests for student interns: government offices, banks, small businesses, and major companies such as IBM and Textron requested Bryant interns.[19]

Students also chose internships with Rhode Island public interest organizations which needed accountants' services. Professor Michael Filippelli, in cooperation with Cap Henry Frank, the director of Accountants for Public Interest (a non-profit group), set up internships for seventy-two Bryant accounting students in twenty-nine agencies. These agencies represented a range of community activities—among them, the Rhode Island Mime Theatre, the Grey Panthers, Rhode Island Early Childhood Research Center, and the YWCA.[20]

At first, students worked ten hours a week, but by the mid-eighties, Pollard was developing a structure for the internship which enabled the student to be in the work environment for a longer, more intensive period. The student now worked full-time in a block of weeks before the semester began and also after the semester ended. Each student was advised by a faculty member, met fellow interns in seminars to discuss problems in the workplace, kept a daily work log, and wrote a final paper on some aspect of the learning experience. At least once during the semester, the student was visited at work by the faculty member who sat down with the intern and supervisor to talk over performance.[21]

Students found that a corporate culture existed for which no textbook had fully prepared them. Susan Sheplak, who interned in the

Warwick, Rhode Island, Filene's personnel department, said the experience enabled her to see the different facets of that kind of work.[22] Sharon Gederman, an intern at Rhode Island Hospital Trust Bank, put training program data into a computer and evaluated new software the bank was considering. She learned that everything had to be planned a year ahead of time.[23]

The student usually endured a period of testing. David Kaiser, an intern in management at General Motors, described the situation when he first went on the job:

> Of course, when I first entered the program, I knew nothing of the workers and they knew nothing of me. As I approached and observed them, they saw me as just another member of management. They were often suspicious of me, wondering why I was watching them. I soon realized that psychology is vital when working in such an environment. The employees thought I was appraising their work habits. . . . Therefore, I made it a point to explain to everyone I encountered that I was a college student, not a performance appraiser. This helped to open the communication lines. . . .[24]

Professor Pollard was pleased with the students' successful performance as reported by their employers: "Out there," she said, "they shine."[25] With the 1986 strategic plan, *The Quality Difference*, Bryant reaffirmed its commitment to internships by establishing the Bryant College Career Experience Program (BRYCEP) to coordinate these endeavors with the Career Services Office.

Another way Bryant sought to cooperate with the business community was through its expansion of services to businesses. The Center for Management Development had been initiated in 1973–74 by Harry Evarts, with Philip Graf as its first director. By the 1980s, under the center's second director, Timothy Sullivan, over 400 professional continuing education programs were offered each year—seminars, non-credit courses, in-company training programs, special programs on taxation, and a CPA review course. These programs provided professional training to over 7,000 upper- and middle-level managers and executives throughout the Northeast. In 1985, Bryant's center ranked as one of the five largest in New England.[26]

The center's strength was in its ability to deliver programs on innovative, timely subjects using nationally known training professionals. In the 1980s, its principal program areas were management and supervisory development, communications, and computer training. Both Bryant College faculty and external consultants conducted the center's programs.

An advisory council, made up of people who were representative of the organizations the center served, assisted the administrative staff in planning and program selection. In addition to taking the advice of the council, the center's administrators also sought out seminar leaders and consultants to determine appropriate program offerings. Their rule of thumb was that the programs had to be practical and provide professional development skills currently useful.[27]

An entirely new service—one designed just for small businesses—was begun at Bryant College in November 1982. The federal government encouraged educational institutions to set up training programs for managers of small businesses. Research showed that 85 percent of business start-ups failed within the first five years; however, 85 percent of small businesses succeeded if the managers had been in training programs. James Hague, a district director of the Small Business Administration, worked with Stanley Kozikowski at Bryant College in applying to the federal government for a grant to start a Small Business Development Center. At that time there were only twenty-four such programs in the nation and none in Rhode Island. The Small Business Administration recognized that Bryant College's outstanding reputation in business education made the school an excellent candidate to operate such a program. Bryant received the grant, becoming the first private college in the nation to oversee a Small Business Development Center.[28]

Bryant's program became fully operational shortly after the first director, Douglas Jobling, assumed the post in June 1983. The center's mission was to assist small businesses in Rhode Island by offering consulting and training services. The objective was to reach businesses which could not afford to hire consultants or pay for expensive training programs. Bryant invited experts in specific businesses to serve as consultants. They were paid a small honorarium by the government; the businesses paid nothing. An advisory council, made up of heads of successful small businesses, queried business leaders all over the state on pertinent topics. Director Jobling and his staff then designed the seminars along the lines recommended by the advisory council. Seminar participants paid as little as $15 to $30, just enough so that the service could be run on a break-even basis. Bryant paid the expenses of housing the program, thereby sharing costs about equally with the federal government. In 1984 the state of Rhode Island also began contributing funds to the center, a clear indication that Bryant's services were valued.

Several satellite offices were established to make the program more accessible—at the South Providence Opportunities Industrialization Center in downtown Providence, Newport, Woonsocket, and the University of Rhode Island. Another new development was the emphasis on international trade: research services were built up to provide client companies with information about potential markets in the international arena and to define the opportunities and obstacles related to each market.[29]

Bryant found that having the Rhode Island Small Business Development Center on its campus brought many more business people to the campus than ever before, made them aware of its faculty (many of whom were SBDC consultants), and helped in the placement of student interns and Bryant graduates in the business community. The consultants enjoyed the challenge of helping small business owners solve tough problems and grow. Hundreds of small businesses throughout Rhode

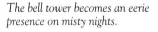

The bell tower becomes an eerie presence on misty nights.

Island benefited substantially from the program.

These external relations were developing at the same time internal relations were changing. Throughout the nation, college administrators in the 1980s became aware of a change in the relationship of the student to the institution. Now, it seemed as if the student had a consumer relationship to the college or university that he or she chose. It was almost as if the student had a contract–the college catalog and the student handbook. The student promised to fulfill the requirements of the contract and he or she expected faculty and administrators to do the same. The student as consumer paid a high price and was determined to receive a quality product–an excellent education. College administrators everywhere had to keep this "new student" in mind and structure educational opportunities in order to satisfy such a sophisticated consumer.[30]

Often this meant offering information college administrators would not have expected to provide in earlier times. Students wanted education to help them make many kinds of decisions in their lives. There was, for example, a growing concern about health issues. The college responded to the needs of this new generation of health-conscious students by establishing a health education program in 1982. Noreen Mattis, a nurse and health education professional who headed the program, spent about 50 percent of her time counseling individuals on personal health problems and about 50 percent offering programs. Often the programs were planned in response to a resident assistant's request for information on a topic of concern to students in a dormitory. Topics students wished to discuss ranged from chemical substance abuse to human sexuality to health and nutrition. Sometimes Mattis offered programs to alert students to recent research data on a health problem. She also acted as a resource to faculty, lecturing in classes and maintaining a lending library of health information materials for faculty and students. The theme of all these efforts was that the individual should take responsibility for his or her own health.[31]

Students took the initiative in developing their own cultural, recreational and athletic activities. In the athletic program, students organized their own teams; in fact, the intramural sports program was almost totally run by students. Sometimes a group formed a team because they had been freshmen together in one wing of a dormitory and they wanted to continue to have an activity together. Sometimes students from the same geographical area formed teams. Intramural teams usually did not have coaches; they chose students to be the captains, and used catchy names, like "The Zoo Crew," or "Suite Dreams."[32]

Varsity teams had coaches paid by the college. In 1981, the Indians, Bryant's varsity basketball team, became a charter member of the Northeast 8 Conference which played in NCAA Division II national tournaments. In 1982 and 1983, the Indians added Division I teams, the University of Rhode Island and Brown University, to the regular season schedule. They also travelled outside of New England–in 1985, to Alaska to play against the University of Alaska at Fairbanks and at Anchorage. Men's varsity teams also competed in baseball, bowling, cross-country, golf, tennis, track, soccer, and volleyball. Women's varsity teams competed in basketball, cross-country, golf, tennis, track, soccer, and volleyball and began to build up a notable record.[33]

Bryant's Multipurpose Activities Center (right). Below, fraternities stage the annual "Teeter-Totterathon". Opposite, students play "oozeball"– a Bryant original.

In addition to these intramural and varsity teams, students formed clubs for hockey, karate, lacrosse, rugby, and frisbee. Although non-varsity, these clubs competed with teams from other colleges. The clubs were supported by funds from the student senate.

For all of these sports, the college provided equipment. Personal items, such as shoes, the athletic department bought from major suppliers at a discount and sold to students at a reduced price. No pressure was put on students to participate; and the athletic department never scheduled games during class time. The college also endeavored to provide excellent facilities for sports. The multi-purpose activities building (affectionately called "The MAC") was finished in 1981 and provided courts for basketball, volleyball, tennis, badminton, and soccer. Also featured were five racquetball-handball courts and a large multi-sports arena that could be used for roller-skating, among other sports.[34]

Ninety percent of the student body participated in some athletic activity. The popularity of the athletic program can be understood in part when one considers that the campus was in a rural setting without easy access to an urban center where other leisure activities would be offered. Debbie Turner, a student who managed a hockey league, said that sports offered students a chance to meet people they would not otherwise meet and have some fun. "Most important," she said, "It's free!"[35]

In addition to the sports offered through the athletic department, students, faculty, staff, and town residents participated in TAP (The Alternative Program). Started by Normand Parenteau, a student activities administrator, TAP offered six-week courses in such subjects as modern dance, self-defense, aerobics, photography, and calligraphy. Fees were $10 to $20, just enough to give the instructor some compensation. Instructors were often students, but sometimes they were staff, faculty, or townspeople. A course was offered when someone wanted to teach it and enough people signed up to take it.[36]

A student programming board had been organized by the student senate at the end of the seventies. Bryant had seventy clubs and organizations, and a coordinating body to plan events was a necessity. A monthly publication, *Programming News*, listed events such as the following: a play, a trip to Boston, a make-your-own-pizza party, a workshop on test anxiety, and a lecture on world events.

In the eighties, students continued to enjoy cultural events, and cultural opportunities were more abundant than in earlier decades. The 1985 strategic plan, *Designs for Quality*, recommended that freshmen be provided with transportation to travel to cultural events off campus. This recommendation was soon implemented. On campus, the Bryant Players, a student-run artistic enterprise, offered theatrical productions. The Bryant Community Chorus attracted participants with "something to sing about." The Performing Arts Series was expanded and included a variety of events—orchestral concerts, Shakespearean productions, modern drama, jazz concerts, and dance programs. For a small admittance fee, people from the Smithfield community attended, along with students, faculty, and staff.

College administrators sought ways to develop further opportunities for students to learn leadership skills and broaden their experiences outside the classroom. The Strategic Planning Committee had recommended that deliberate efforts be made to formalize such opportunities in a "Learning for Leadership Program." The committee members also wanted Bryant students to be knowledgeable about major social issues. They looked for ways to bring into focus a concern for international problems. These were challenges students, faculty, and administrators continued to work on. The 1985 strategic plan also called for funds to bring business leaders to the campus for forums, seminars, and talks with students.

Bryant students had always had part-time jobs. On the East Side, getting such jobs was not a problem because of the proximity of the city's businesses. Students on the rural campus in Smithfield, however, had a difficult time finding part-time employment. In 1979, the college recognized the need to help students find part-time jobs and established the Student Employment Program. A coordinator, David Brooks, worked with students and off-campus employers to match student interests and talents with company needs. The office also administered the College Work-Study Program (CWSP) which provided funding not only to students who worked at the college but also to those who worked for nonprofit organizations. Under this arrangement a student receiving financial aid worked off-campus for a nonprofit organization—such as the public library or a hospital—and was paid in part by the organization, in part by a federal grant.[37] Sometimes, students who were receiving no financial aid but still had a hard time making ends meet worked in an office where they gained valuable experience as well as a needed salary.

According to Bryant tradition, job placement after graduation was a concern of the college. In earlier times, the staff had screened employers, interviewed graduating seniors, then picked one or two seniors to go to a job interview. In the seventies and eighties, the approach was different. The Career Services Office became an equal opportunity referral service. Career planning began as soon as a student chose a major, and individual and group counseling helped students narrow career interests, clarify values, and pinpoint specific jobs they wanted. The staff then prepared all interested students to meet potential employers. Students attended workshops covering such topics as resume-writing, interviewing skills, and job search skills. The staff also contacted alumni willing to talk to students about their work so that students could get some "inside" information on particular careers. All available jobs were posted and students took the initiative in selecting the jobs they wanted and setting up interviews.[38]

Bryant students made up a community that was a microcosm of the larger world. They experienced all the stress, financial constraints, peer pressures, and in many cases, job pressures, that graduates experienced outside the campus. The tendency in the seventies and eighties was to view students as young men and women with adult responsibilities.[39] Administrators in student life offices saw their objective as out-of-classroom education. For example, Edward Golden, dean of student life, led a faculty-student committee on discipline. Students gained valuable experience acting as arbiters of complaints and developed management skills.[40]

Student involvement in college committees continued at a high level throughout the eighties. In their jobs, in their choice of sports and recreation, and in their choice of academic programs, students felt a growing sense of power to direct their lives at the college.

Faculty involvement also continued to increase, with quality in the educational experience the primary concern. The faculty union—the Federation—concentrated on ensuring continued academic freedom and professional integrity. Wary of making dollars the yardstick to measure education, faculty insisted on forming a committee to monitor the actual, in-class quality of instruction. Faculty also crossed swords with proponents of the plan to make department chairs "academic managers." (This was a recommendation of the Strategic Planning Committee.) Faculty were used to a democratic system wherein the chairperson was one among equals and decisions about procedures were made by the entire department.[41]

Faculty, students, and administrators were all immersed in the decisions that affected a college that was growing, both in its programs and in its physical plant. Resources to finance this expansion were the concern of all and the daily responsibility of the administration and the board of trustees.

From the mid-seventies to the mid-eighties, the college made significant improvements in its and administrative practices which led to dramatic increases in its capabilities. Without this, the expansion of facilities and programs would have been difficult. Among these innovations were sophisticated cash management procedures and an effective master plan for continually "renewing" campus facilities as they aged. The college's officers also devised tax exempt financing packages and accomplished an eight fold increase in endowment funds.[42]

Funds for the expansion came from bond issues and from Bryant's supporters in the wider community. In the eighties, the development staff (now part of the Institutional Advancement Division) was expanded. The 1979–80 annual fund exceeded its goal with total contributions of $206,000.[43] This sum was even higher than the total of the 1978–79 annual fund which had won the United States Steel/Council for the Advancement and Support of Education Award. The three-year corporate campaign which was begun in 1978 to build the multi-purpose activities center was highly successful. The total raised in 1980–81 was $514,000; in 1983–84, $738,000; and in 1984–85, $704,000. In 1985–86, the institutional advancement staff confidently set as its year's goal a million dollars: it raised over a million–$1,152,499.[44]

These donations to the college were tangible evidence of Bryant's good reputation, just as the dedicated efforts of faculty, staff, and students expressed the spirit of optimism on campus in the 1980s. People at Bryant were looking ahead to the future when many educators at other colleges were thinking of retrenchment.

There was an excitement about the coming decades based on the realization that education was becoming a life-long enterprise. Individual growth and creativity would be increasingly necessary in a rapidly changing society. Bryant alumni might very well expect to have four or five

The Student Employment Program helped students find part-time jobs while in school.

different careers. To prepare students for such a life presented a challenge to those at the college in charge of undergraduate and graduate curricula. President O'Hara explained, "The modern corporate world is extraordinarily demanding and we have to respond."[45]

The development of educational programs rather than expansion was the objective.

Growth in undergraduate enrollment was not expected to continue: demographic research projected a 25 percent drop in the number of United States high school graduates from 1972 to 1992. Rhode Island expected a 49 percent drop. President O'Hara believed that growth would occur in executive training programs and in specialized services to the wider community. For example, the Small Business Development Center could grow into a service which would coordinate information and training seminars for people in the area who owned small businesses.[46]

The history of Bryant's first 125 years reveals that a close relationship with business was a continuing trend at the college. From the very beginning in 1863, Bryant sought to involve business leaders in the work of the college by hiring them to teach, by honoring them at graduation ceremonies, and by sending Bryant graduates to them. In the fifties, Harry Jacobs and Gertrude Hochberg had initiated the annual Business Management Institute; Professor Joseph Santos had offered special short-term courses to meet the needs of specific businesses. The graduate program in the evening was set up to help working people in the state become more effective in their businesses and professions. The Center for Management Development, started in the seventies, and the Small Business Development Center, begun in the eighties, provided a more extensive means of serving the business community. The internship program also forged links with for-profit enterprises in New England. Something new in the 1980s was the attention given to serving non-profit endeavors, both in sending interns to them and in inviting their managers to Center for Management Development and Small Business Development Center seminars.

In the 1970s and 1980s, the liberal arts became an increasingly important component of a Bryant education. Here, Prof. Gaytha Langlois brings a biology lesson to life.

The college continued to anticipate changes in technology in the business world and to adapt its programs to meet students' needs arising from these changes. In the eighties, however, the faculty and administration anticipated that the student would need a broader education—a knowledge of history, philosophy, literature, sociology, psychology, science, and art—to be an effective person both at work and in other activities. Students now took about 50 percent of their courses in professional subjects and 50 percent in liberal arts subjects. This was a situation not glimpsed by the founders, Bryant, Stratton, and Mason, nor even by Harry Jacobs. The college had redefined its educational goals.

Another change in the way Bryant organized the college experience took place in the three decades of the sixties, seventies, and eighties. Until then, the college's history had been dominated by a few individuals. Beginning in the 1960s, faculty, then students, demanded and obtained a share in decision-making power. With the advent of college presidents who were not members of the Jacobs family, the board of trustees asserted its right to set policy. President O'Hara made sure that all constituencies were represented in planning for the future. An important aspect of the growing sense of self-determination at Bryant emerged in the seventies and eighties when students obtained a greater degree of control over residential life, forming their own rules of conduct and creating their own recreational and cultural groups. The evolution of a democratic system of governance which encouraged initiative and responsibility was an important twentieth century development in the college's history.

In these ways, Bryant College continuously strengthened its commitment to its primary constituency, its students, anticipating their needs and shaping programs to serve them. In the nineteenth and early twentieth centuries, administrators and faculty had asked how they could best prepare students for their life's work. In the eighties, the Bryant community asked a more universal question: What do our students need to learn in order to live a meaningful life? This was the concern which guided the college through the process of redefining its mission.

The Bryant Center, below and opposite, opened in 1986, became the principal gathering place for the college community.

125 Years and Beyond

THE FALL OF 1987 marked the beginning of Bryant's 125th anniversary celebration. At convocation on September 16, a Bryant anniversary flag was carried from the college's birthplace at 56 Westminster Street to the old East Side campus, and then to the new campus in Smithfield. The event symbolized Bryant's development over a century and a quarter. The college had evolved from a proprietary, skills-oriented school in the nineteenth century to a more traditional business college in the mid-twentieth century and finally, in the 1970s and 1980s, to a comprehensive institution awarding graduate degrees and providing extensive services to the business community.

If Harry Jacobs could have come back to stand by the archway on the Smithfield campus in 1987, he would have been astonished at his college's new architecture. Even Bryant graduates of only a few years past were impressed by the new buildings opened just prior to the college's anniversary year. The new Bryant Center, completed in 1986, provided the hoped-for gathering place for the Bryant community. A new freshman dormitory, also finished in 1986, enabled the college to make available to incoming students a comfortable and attractive residence. The Koffler Technology Center, finished and dedicated in the fall of the anniversary year, was part new construction, part renovation of the former student center. It provided a whole new world of computing technology for students, faculty, administrators, and regional corporations.

Just before its 125th year, the college began to reap some of the first fruits of the recently instituted strategic planning process. The 1986 strategic plan, *The Quality Difference*, had recommended increased levels of support for faculty research. Under the new vice president for academic affairs, James Robinson, and Michael Patterson, associate vice president, faculty were encouraged by the opportunity to be released from teaching one of their courses and by grants to support their research and writing. Many of them responded by producing scholarly publications which added to their own reputation and to Bryant's. President O'Hara looked forward to establishing two additional endowed professorships– one in management and one in marketing–and to expanding the faculty each year through 1991.

Plans for new opportunities for students were being implemented.

To inaugurate the 125th anniversary year, Bryant students, faculty and staff traced the route from the college's earlier locations in Providence to the Smithfield campus.

Pictured at Bryant's 125th Anniversary Jubilee Ball are (left to right) Executive Vice President William E. Trueheart, Special Assistant to the President Priscilla Angelo, President O'Hara, and Vice President for Student Affairs Leslie LaFond.

As a result of the 1985 strategic plan, *Designs for Quality*, freshmen began to take part in a special mentor program which brought them off campus to a variety of cultural and community events. A Senior Challenge was being planned to give students an opportunity to integrate the knowledge they had gained in their four years at Bryant. Outstanding leaders from the world of business as well as widely-read authors and critics came to the campus to speak and conduct seminars—notable among them were David Halberstam, author of *The Best and the Brightest*; the Rev. Leon Sullivan, creator of the Sullivan principles for American businesses operating in South Africa; and Letitia Baldrige, whom *Time* magazine had called "the arbiter of America's manners."

In 1986, the administration expanded to meet the needs of the growing college. A Bryant trustee, William E. Trueheart, former associate secretary to Harvard University in the Office of Governing Boards, was selected to fill the newly-created position of executive vice president. Trueheart's leadership as chief operating officer at Bryant allowed the president more time to spend off campus, communicating Bryant's mission and message to the larger community. This was an important duty as Bryant became an institution with national interests.

Strategic planning at Bryant had pointed to the need for these programmatic and administrative changes. In addition, the ongoing planning process provided clear goals for the college as it looked ahead to the educational challenges of the next century.

President O'Hara expressed the sense of excitement and expectation that was in the air during the 125th anniversary year when he said:

> This is an historic moment in the long and distinguished history of Bryant College. Our analysis of demographics, of America's business needs, of the future of higher education and our place in it—all of these have gone into the momentous decision to attain a new level of excellence for Bryant. If you are proud of Bryant today, you will be electrified as the years unfold.

All documents are contained in the Bryant College archives in the Edith M. Hodgson Memorial Library unless otherwise noted. All tape-recorded interviews are in the Bryant College archives, unless otherwise noted. The editors would like to thank everyone who helped make this history possible by commenting on manuscript drafts, identifying photographs, or sharing memories of Bryant.

CHAPTER I

1. S. S. Packard, "The Evolution of Business Colleges" (abstract of opening speech), *Proceedings of the International Congress of Education of the World's Columbian Exposition*, Chicago, July 25–28, 1883 (New York: National Education Association, 1894), 788.

2. Edwin G. Knepper, *A History of Business Education in the United States* (Bowling Green, Ohio: Edward Brothers, Inc., 1941), 50.

3. Elyce J. Rotella, *From Home to Office: U.S. Women at Work, 1870–1930* (Ann Arbor: University of Michigan Research Press, 1981), 61.

4. Cheesman A. Herrick, *The Meaning and Practice of Commercial Education* (New York: The MacMillan Company, 1904), 200.

5. Ibid.

6. *Dictionary of American Biography* 18: 395.

7. Knepper, *History*, 64.

8. *National Cyclopedia* 3: 72.

9. Knepper, *History*, 64.

10. Quoted in Knepper, *History*, 51.

11. *Bryant, Stratton and Mason's National Business College* (Providence, Rhode Island: Pierce and Budlow, Printers, 1865), 4. (Rhode Island Historical Society Library.)

12. "Bryant and Stratton Opening Agreement." New York, January 14, 1863.

13. *Report Upon the Census of Rhode Island, 1865* (Providence: Providence Press, 1867) p. 25, Table XVI.

14. *Bryant, Stratton and Mason's National Business College* (Circular, 1865), 24.

15. Ibid.

16. Ibid.

17. Ibid.

18. Ibid., 14. See also Bryant and Stratton's Mercantile College certificate, August 20, 1864.

19. Knepper, *History*, 32.

20. *Bryant, Stratton and Mason's National Business College* (Circular, 1865), 8.

21. Ibid., 14.

22. Ibid., 18.

23. Herrick, *Meaning*, 185.

24. Garrett D. Byrnes, "A Long Trail to the Groves of Academe," *Providence Journal*, April 23, 1972.

25. Nelson Gulski, "A History of Business Education as Seen by a Bryant College Administrator," 7. (Unpublished manuscript in the President's Office, Bryant College.)

26. T. B. Stowell, *Methods of a Business College* (Providence, Rhode Island, and Boston: L. Barta and Company, Printers, 1892).

27. Margery W. Davies, *Woman's Place Is at the Typewriter: Office Work and Office Workers, 1870–1930* (Philadelphia: Temple University Press, 1982), 37.

28. Ibid.

29. Rhode Island Bureau of Industrial Statistics, *Third Annual Report, 1889*. Table VI, "Average Annual Weekly Wages of Each Occupation."

30. Rotella, *From Home to Office*, 69.

31. Advertisement labelled "The Dictation Phonograph," *Providence Board of Trade Journal*, 1908 (end page of the February issue).

32. *Providence. Bryant and Stratton Business College, Shorthand and Typewriting School* (Catalog), 1895. (Rhode Island Historical Society.)

33. *Providence. Bryant and Stratton Business College Register*, vol. xv, no. 15 (1885–6).

34. *How the Methods of Business Are Taught in Providence* (Providence, Rhode Island: R. A. Reid, Printers, n.d.). (Rhode Island Historical Society Library.)

35. *The History of Rhode Island and Providence Plantations: Biographical* (New York: American Historical Society, 1920), 435.

36. Gulski, "A History of Business Education," 7.

37. *How the Methods of Business Are Taught in Providence*.

38. *Providence Directory*, 1916, p. 1278.

39. Virginia Conroy, "Providence Was Great Show Town," *Rhode Island Year Book* (Providence: Rhode Island Yearbook Foundation, 1970), p. H-182.

40. *Chronology and Documentary Handbook of the State of Rhode Island*, edited by Robert I. Vexler (Dobbs Ferry, N.Y.: Oceana Publications, 1979) 134–136. Reprint from *New England Magazine*, October 1907, 131–160.

41. "Rhode Island Wheelmen – Pavement Pioneers," *Rhode Island Yearbook* (Providence: Rhode Island Yearbook Foundation, 1968), H-127.

42. Henry Foley, interview with author, July 29, 1985, tape-recorded at Bryant College, 1: 391. (Harry Jacobs recounted to Foley his early work experiences.)

43. Byrnes, "A Long Trail" and "He Left Others Breathless," *Evening Bulletin* (Providence), October 25, 1961; "Official Biography of Dr. Henry L. Jacobs," (now contained in Harry Jacobs' folder, Bryant College Archives): Gertrude Hochberg, *News Bulletin*, October 1961 (Harry Jacobs' folder, Bryant College Archives).

44. Ethel Barmingham, interview with author, 1982, tape-recorded in East Greenwich, Rhode Island, Rhode Island Clerical Workers' Tapes. (Rhode Island Historical Society Library.)

45. *Business Training.* "Published in the Interests of the Students and Friends of Rhode Island Commercial School," vol. 1 no. 5 (August 1914).

46. Ibid.

47. *Providence Journal*, May 25, 1916, p. 3.

48. *Providence Journal*, May 19, 1916, p. 14.

49. J. O. Malott, "Commercial Education in 1924–26," Department of the Interior, Bureau of Education, Bulletin Number 4, (Washington: United States Government Printing Office, 1928), 3.

50. *Providence Journal*, August 12, 1916, p. 8.

51. *Evening Bulletin* (Providence): March 23, 1949.

52. Gulski, "A History of Business Education," 9, 10.

53. *Studying Nights For Higher Salaries* (Providence: Bryant and Stratton Commercial School, 1919), 15.

CHAPTER 2

1. *Bryant and Stratton Commercial School, Providence, Fifty-eighth Yearbook, 1919–1920*, p. 7.

2. Frank M. Phillips, *Statistics of Private Commercial Business Schools, 1924–25*, United States Department of the Interior, Bureau of Education, Bulletin Number 14, "Enrollments in Commercial Curriculum, 1914–1924" (Washington: U.S. Government Printing Office, 1926), 3.

3. Ibid.

4. Nelson Gulski, "A History of Business Education as Seen by a Bryant College Administrator," p. 11 (President's Office, Bryant College.)

5. *Providence Magazine* 36: 3 (March 1925): 106–108.

6. *Providence Journal*, March 29, 1924.

7. *Providence Journal*, March 12, 1925, p. 19.

8. *Providence Journal*, August 17, 1929, p. 5.

9. *Providence Journal*, August 10, 1930, p. 9.

10. Joseph Santos, interview with author, August 1, 1985, tape-recorded at Bryant College, 1: 634; *Providence Journal*, August 15, 1931, p. 20.

11. *Earning Power* VII (December 1924), no. 1. (Rhode Island Historical Society Library.)

12. *Earning Power* VII (September 1925), no. 4. (Rhode Island Historical Society Library.)

13. *Earning Power* VII (March 1925), no. 2. (Rhode Island Historical Society Library.)

14. Nelson Gulski, interview with author, July 27, 1985, tape-recorded in Attleboro, Massachusetts, 1: 002.

15. *Bryant and Stratton College of Business Administration, 1927–28* (Providence: Bryant and Stratton College, 1927), 32–33.

16. *Bryant and Stratton College for Business Training, 1924–25* (Providence: Bryant and Stratton College, 1924), 79.

17. *Providence Journal*, August 17, 1929, p. 5 and August 10, 1930, p. 9.

18. Harry Jacobs, letter to trustees, October 23, 1961 (Henry Loeb Jacobs folder, Bryant College Archives.)

19. Nelson Gulski, interview, 1: 130.

20. Nelson Gulski, written communication, March 1986.

21. Gulski, interview, 1: 223.

22. George Craig, interview with author, August 22, 1985, tape-recorded in Warwick, Rhode Island, 1: 028.

23. Gardner Jacobs, interview with author, July 19, 1985, tape-recorded in North Kingstown, Rhode Island, 1: 121.

24. Ibid.

25. *Bryant-Stratton News* 4: 3 (November 29, 1933), 1.

26. *Bryant College, Catalog, 1936–37,* p. 15.

27. Ibid.

28. *Providence Journal*, May 29, 1937, p. 4.

29. *Bryant College, Catalog, 1937–38.*

30. Gulski, "History," 12.

31. "Streets of the City," radio program on WEAN, the radio service of the *Providence Journal-Bulletin*, August 1, 1966. (Bryant College Archives.)

32. *Providence Journal*, September 23, 1935.

33. Gulski, "History," 13.

34. Nelson Gulski, "In His Own Words: Remarks by Dean Gulski on the Occasion of Commencement," June 3, 1972, *Bryant Review,* Fall 1972, p. 5.

35. *Providence Journal*, January 5, 1939.

36. *Providence Journal*, August 24, 1938.

37. *Evening Bulletin* (Providence), July 21, 1929, p. 17.

38. *Providence Journal*, July 7, 1940, p. 15.

CHAPTER 3

1. *Providence Journal*, August 8, 1942, p. 5; and August 7, 1943, p. 8. *Evening Bulletin* (Providence), August 4, 1944, p. 8.

2. Gertrude Hochberg, personal communication, August 1985.

3. *Calling All G.I.s: Educational Opportunities for Men and Women Veterans of World War II at Bryant College* (Providence, R.I., n.d.) (Rhode Island Historical Society Library.)

4. Gardner Jacobs, interview with author, July 19, 1985, tape-recorded in North Kingstown, Rhode Island, 2: 250.

5. *Evening Bulletin* (Providence), March 23, 1949.

6. Nelson Gulski, interview with author, July 27, 1985, tape-recorded in Attleboro, Massachusetts, 1: 250.

7. Ibid.

8. Herbert McLaughlin, interview with author, July 22, 1985, tape-recorded at Bryant College, 1: 070.

9. Dominic Falcone, interview with author, July 22, 1985, tape-recorded in Providence, Rhode Island, 1: 048.

10. Jacobs, interview, 2: 232.

11. *Providence Journal*, August 3, 1947.

12. Ibid.

13. *Evening Bulletin* (Providence), March 23, 1949.

14. Ibid.

15. Jacobs, interview, 1: 105.

16. *Providence Journal*, March 23, 1949, p. 8.

17. Ibid.

18. *Evening Bulletin* (Providence), March 16, 1949, p. 1.

19. *Providence Journal*, April 30, 1949, p. 3. An Act to Incorporate the Bryant College of Business Administration, H14. State of Rhode Island and Providence Plantations, January Session, A.D. 1949.

20. Nelson Gulski, written communication, June 25, 1987.

21. Ibid.

22. Ibid.

23. Gulski, interview, 1: 264. Joseph Santos, interview with author, August 1, 1985, tape-recorded at Bryant College, 2: 224.

24. Nelson Gulski, "A History of Business Education As Seen by a Bryant College Administrator," p. 14.

25. Gertrude Hochberg, interview with author, July 16, 1985, tape-recorded in Providence, Rhode Island, 1: 073.

26. Ibid., 1: 008 and 073.

27. Ibid.

28. Ibid., 1: 467.

29. *Providence Journal*, June 19, 1977, A17.

30. Ibid., 1, 385.

31. Ibid., 2, 020.

32. Harry Jacobs, Speech to the Interfaith Council Brotherhood Conference, March 26, 1953. (Folder, "Henry L. Jacobs' Speeches," Bryant College Archives.)

33. *First Annual Business Management Institute.* October 27, 1950. (Leaflet, Bryant College Archives); and *Second Annual Business Management Institute.* October 25, 1951. (Leaflet, Bryant College Archives). See also *Bryant College Bulletin*, October 1951, p. 1 and 3.

34. *Evening Bulletin* (Providence), August 4, 1944, p. 8 and *Providence Journal*, July 21, 1947, p. 8.

35. *Providence Journal*, August 6, 1949, p. 11.

36. *Bulletin of Bryant College – Alumni Issue*, July 1951, 1952, 1953, 1957.

37. Ibid., 1953.

38. Jacobs, interview, 1: 112.

39. Ibid.

40. Ibid., 136.

41. Joseph Santos, interview, 2: 004.

42. Gulski, "History," 17.

43. Ibid.

44. *Evening Bulletin* (Providence), May 9, 1959, p. 2.

45. George Craig, interview with author, August 22, 1985, tape-recorded in Warwick, Rhode Island, 2: 141.

46. Santos, oral history, 1: 025.

47. Ibid., 1: 133.

48. Ibid., 1: 147.

49. *Bulletin of Bryant College*, Alumni Issue, October 1952.

50. *Providence Journal*, January 25, 1959, N25.

51. Ibid., September 4, 1954, p. 8.

52. Santos, interview, 1: 330, and *Evening Bulletin* (Providence), July 25, 1950.

53. Clarissa Patterson, written communication, August 1986.

54. Ibid.

55. *Providence Journal*, April 22, 1952, p. 8; September 10, 1952, p. 4; April 11, 1951, p. 15; December 9, 1953, p. 4.

56. *Providence Journal*, December 9, 1953; December 19, 1954, S 1, 59; December 18, 1955, p. 53.

57. Falcone, interview, 1: 467.

58. *Providence Journal*, December 12, 1950, p. 5.

59. Lynne Hayden Simonds, interview with author, August 23, 1985, tape-recorded at Bryant College, 1: 045.

60. Philomena Castronovo, telephone interview, December 1985.

61. Ibid.

62. John F. Gillooly, written communication, October 1, 1986.

63. *Bulletin of Bryant College*, October 1953, p. 1.

64. Karl Ericson, interview with author, August 15, 1985, tape-recorded in Providence, Rhode Island, 1: 012.

65. Clarissa Patterson, interview with author, July 24, 1985, tape-recorded at Bryant College, 1: 030.

66. Frank Delmonico, interview with author, July 31, 1985, tape-recorded in Providence, Rhode Island, 1: 045.

67. *Bryant College Bulletin*, Alumni Issue, October 1955.

68. Jacobs, interview, 2: 003; *Evening Bulletin* (Providence), May 14, 1959, p. 1.

69. Jacobs, interview, 2: 228.

CHAPTER 4

1. Gardner Jacobs, interview with author, July 19, 1985, tape-recorded in Warwick, Rhode Island, 1: 010.

2. Henry Foley, interview with author, July 29, 1985, tape-recorded at Bryant College, 2: 081.

3. Jacobs, interview, July 19, 1985, 1: 275 and 402.

4. Ibid., 1: 402.

5. *Providence Journal*, December 13, 1964; Jacobs, interview, 1: 402.

6. *Providence Journal*, February 27, 1966, N4.

7. *Archway*, November 13, 1964.

8. Maurice Clare, telephone conversation, December 21, 1985.

9. Ibid.

10. John F. Gillooly, "Bryant Basketball History," *Bryant Basketball*, (Smithfield: Bryant College, 1985).

11. Maurice Clare, telephone conversation.

12. Ibid.

13. *Evening Bulletin* (Providence), December 8, 1967, p. 1 and April 18, 1969, p. 2.

14. *Providence Journal*, October 2, 1966, N10.

15. Gertrude Hochberg, interview with author, July 16, 1985, tape-recorded in Providence, Rhode Island, 2: 112.

16. *Bulletin of Bryant College*, October 1963; *Archway*, October 25, 1963.

17. Clarissa Patterson, written communication, August 1986.

18. Ibid.

19. *Archway* xxiv, No. 1 (September 27, 1963, p. 1).

20. *Bryant Review*, January 1963 and April 1964; and *Archway*, February 26, 1965.

21. Wallace Camper, interview, December 1985.

22. *Providence Journal*, December 13, 1964.

23. Herbert McLaughlin, interview with author, July 22, 1985, tape-recorded at Bryant College, 1: 417.

24. Frank Delmonico, interview with author, July 31, 1985, tape-recorded at Bryant College, 1: 241.

25. Clarissa Patterson, written communication, August 1986.

26. Draft report by Knight and Gladieux Management Consultants, June 1967, page 51. (Archives of Professor James Ingraham.)

27. Bernard Gladieux to Dr. E. Gardner Jacobs, letter of June 26, 1967. (Archives of Professor James Ingraham.)

28. Ingraham, interview, 1: 406.

29. Ibid.

30. Camper, interview, December 1985.

31. Foley, interview, 1: 422.

32. John A. Radichek, "The Bryant College Faculty Federation," manuscript submitted to a class at the Harvard Business School, April 21, 1972, p. 6 (Archives of Professor James Ingraham.) Katherine Mangan, "I Had to Do Something," *The Chronicle of Higher Education*, May 13, 1987, p. 15 and 25.

33. Foley, interview, 1: 591.

34. Jacobs, interview, 1: 355.

35. Radichek, "The Bryant College Faculty Federation," 7.

36. James Ingraham, letter to Rose Claffey, June 8, 1967. (Archives of Professor James Ingraham.)

37. "Statement of the Board of Trustees of Bryant College, May 12, 1967." (Archives of Professor James Ingraham.)

38. Ingraham, interview, 1: 474.

39. Ratichek, "The Bryant College Faculty Federation," 9; James Ingraham, private communication, January 1986.

40. McLaughlin, interview, 2: 012.

41. Clarissa Patterson, interview with author, July 24, 1985, tape-recorded at Bryant College, 2: 296.

42. Ingraham, interview, 1: 540.

43. "Agreement Made At Providence, Rhode Island, as of the 22nd day of April 1968, between Bryant College of Business Administration . . . and the Bryant Faculty Federation, Local 1769," p. 1. (Archives of Professor James Ingraham.)

44. "Statement of the Bryant Faculty Federation Regarding Non-Academic Clerical Duties of Faculty Members." (Archives of Professor James Ingraham.)

45. "Agreement Made Between the Bryant Faculty Federation and Bryant College of Business Administration on this 19th day of December 1967. (Archives of Professor James Ingraham.)

46. *Bulletin of Bryant College*, April 1967.

47. "Declaration of the Bryant Faculty Federation," (n.d.) (Archives of Professor James Ingraham.)

48. Re-Evaluation Report, 1967, "Encouragement and Help for Faculty Growth." (Archives of Professor James Ingraham.)

49. *Archway*, January 10, 1968.

50. Ibid.

51. *Archway*, editorial, March 15, 1968.

52. *Archway*, December 3, 1968.

53. *Archway*, editorial, May 2, 1969.

54. *Archway*, May 9, 1969.

55. William Smith, telephone conversation, December 1985; Philomena Castronovo, telephone conversation, December 1985.

56. *Archway*, November 7, 1969.

57. Ibid., October 4, 1969.

58. Ibid., November 7, 1969.

59. Ibid., March 6, 1970.

60. Lynn Hayden Simonds, interview with author, August 23, 1985, tape-recorded at Bryant College, 1: 302.

61. *Archway*, March 6, 1970.

62. Ibid., March 26, 1970.

63. Ibid., April 17, 1970.

64. Simonds, interview, 1: 609.

65. *Archway*, February 20, 1970.

66. Sol Lebovitz, interview with author, August 9, 1985, tape-recorded in Barrington, Rhode Island, 1: 103.

67. Ibid., 129.

68. Clarissa Patterson, written communication, December 1985.

69. *Archway*, October 27, 1967.

70. Simonds, interview, 1: 272.

71. *Archway*, April 17, 1970.

72. Ibid., May 7, 1970.

73. Simonds, interview, 1: 556.

74. Roy Nelson, interview with author, August 20, 1985, tape-recorded at Bryant College, 1: 656

CHAPTER 5

1. Frank Delmonico, interview with author, July 31, 1985, tape-recorded in Providence, Rhode Island, 1: 371.

2. Ibid., 1: 468.

3. Gardner Jacobs, interview with author, July 19, 1985, tape-recorded in Providence, Rhode Island, 1: 206.

4. Gertrude Hochberg, interview with author, July 16, 1985, tape-recorded in Providence, Rhode Island, 1: 206.

5. Delmonico, interview, 1: 371.

6. Jacobs, interview, 1: 038–365.

7. *Providence Journal*, October 24, 1967.

8. Delmonico, interview, 1: 371.

9. Ibid., 543.

10. Ibid., 461.

11. Ibid., 2: 165

12. Press release. "Bryant Negotiates Sale of Property to Brown." April 1969. (Bryant College Archives.)

13. Delmonico, interview, 2: 242.

14. Ibid., 1: 543.

15. *Archway*, April 17, 1970.

16. Ibid., November 8, 1968.

17. Robert Hillier, interview with author, December 11, 1985, tape-recorded in Princeton, New Jersey, 1:064.

18. Ibid., 1:064.

19. Delmonico, interview, 1:044.

20. William Smith, telephone conversation, December 21, 1985.

21. Hillier, interview, 1:064. See also press release by Schuyler Hoslett, February 21, 1969. (Bryant College Archives.)

22. Delmonico, interview, 2:045.

23. Lynne Hayden Simonds, interview with author, August 23, 1985, tape-recorded at Bryant College, 1:600.

24. Hillier, interview, 1:217.

25. Ibid.

26. Ibid.

27. *Providence Journal*, April 30, 1971.

28. Hillier, interview, 1:200.

29. John Hannon, interview with author, July 24, 1985, tape-recorded at Bryant College, 1:080, 119, 162.

30. Ibid., 1:239–490; 2:001, 147.

31. Ibid., 1:192.

32. Hillier, interview, 1:478.

33. Ibid., 560.

34. Delmonico, interview, 2:007.

35. Gertrude Hochberg, interview with author, July 26, 1985, tape-recorded in Providence, 1:300.

36. Nelson Gulski, interview with author, July 27, 1985, tape-recorded in Attleboro, Massachusetts, 1:469.

37. Delmonico, interview, 2:071.

38. David Simpson, telephone communication, June 26, 1987.

39. *Providence Journal*, November 22, 1973, p. 23.

40. Hillier, interview, 2:129.

41. Ibid., 1:342.

42. *Archway*, "Special Issue on College Dedication," April 28, 1972. Hillier, interview, 1:270.

43. Roy Nelson, interview with author, August 20, 1985, tape-recorded at Bryant College, 2:001.

44. *Bryant Review*, Summer 1972.

45. Delmonico, interview, 2:273.

46. *Bryant Review*, Winter 1971, statement by President Evarts.

47. *Archway*, "Special Issue on College Dedication," April 28, 1972.

48. Ibid.

49. Peter Barlow, telephone conversation, December 1985.

50. Herbert McLaughlin, interview with author, July 22, 1985, tape-recorded at Bryant College, 2:103.

CHAPTER 6

1. Phil Graf to William O'Hara, "The Future Paper," April 3, 1978, p. 2. (Center for Management Development Archives.)

2. Ibid., 3

3. *Bryant Review*, Winter 1974.

4. Ibid., Spring 1974.

5. Graf, "Future Paper," 3.

6. Wallace Camper, interview with author, Bryant College, December 19, 1985.

7. *Archway*, September 19, 1969.

8. Charles Snyder, interview with author, December 20, 1985.

9. Snyder, interview.

10. Ibid.

11. *Bulletin of Bryant College Graduate School*, December 1977, p. 8.

12. *Bryant Review*, Spring 1977.

13. Sol Lebovitz, interview with author, August 9, 1985, tape-recorded in Barrington, Rhode Island, 1: 430.

14. Gertrude Hochberg, interview with author, July 16, 1985, tape-recorded in Providence, Rhode Island, 1: 522.

15. George Craig, interview with author, August 22, 1985, tape-recorded in Providence, Rhode Island, 1: 382.

16. Francesca M. Cancian, "Rapid Social Change: Women Students in Business Schools," *Social Science Review* 66: 2: 169–183, see p. 175.

17. Jo-Anne Lema, "Fact Book 1984– 85," (Bryant College, Smithfield, Rhode Island, Office of Institutional Research, 1984.) Table A 6, "New Enrollees by Major, Male vs. Female."

18. Peter Barlow, telephone conversation with author, December 1985.

19. Ibid.

20. Roy Nelson, *Bulletin of Bryant College*, Fall 1974, 4–5.

21. *Bryant Success Story* (Smithfield, R.I.: Bryant College, 1979), 2.

22. Nelson, *Bulletin*, 4.

23. Henry Foley, interview with author, July 29, 1985, tape-recorded at Bryant College, 1: 323.

24. Estimate based on a comparison of personnel and faculty listed in the Bryant College Catalogs for 1970 and 1980.

25. Barlow, telephone conversation.

26. Herbert McLaughlin, interview with author, July 22, 1985, tape-recorded at Bryant College, 2: 093.

27. Harry Evarts, conversation with reporters, *Evening Bulletin* (Providence), May 9, 1975.

28. *Providence Sunday Journal*, March 9, 1975, F-13.

29. *Archway*, XXXVIII, 16 (February 2, 1973) pp. 1 and 6.

30. William Haas, interview with author, at Bryant College, August 19, 1986.

31. *Evening Bulletin* (Providence), May 9, 1975.

32. Clarissa Patterson, written communication to author, August 1986.

33. Patterson, interview, 1: 393.

34. Lema, "Fact Book, 1984–85," "Faculty Trends, 1977–81," and "Full-Time Faculty by Race and Sex, 1977–1981."

35. "Community Paper" (Bryant College, loose sheets distributed by striking faculty and students in March 1975.)

36. *Providence Sunday Journal*, March 9, 1975, p. F-13.

37. *Providence Journal*, March 5, 1975, p. 1; March 9, 1975, p. F-1 and March 11, 1975, p. A-1; *Evening Bulletin* (Providence), March 10, 1975, A-1. See also "Community Paper" (sheet published at Bryant College by the strikers).

38. *Providence Journal*, March 5, 1975, p. 1. See also, "Statement of the Bryant College Board of Trustees."

39. Gifford, interview, 2: 001.

40. "Statement of the Bryant College Board of Trustees."

41. Haas, interview, August 19, 1986.

42. William Robinson, interview with author, July 26, 1985, tape-recorded in Providence, Rhode Island, 1: 069 and 197.

43. Barlow, telephone interview.

44. *Fresh Fruit*, (Providence, Rhode Island), October 24, 1975, pp. 1, 4–5.

45. William O'Hara, interview with author, August 8, 1985, tape-recorded at Bryant College, 1: 063.

46. *Providence Journal*, May 15, 1977.

47. "College Mission," Report of the Long-Range Planning Committee, 1979.

48. O'Hara, interview, 1: 104; Ericson, interview, 2: 025.

49. *Evening Bulletin* (Providence), September 27, 1975, p. 1.; *Providence Journal*, November 20, 1975, p. B-4; *Evening Bulletin* (Providence), December 15, 1976, p. D-3.

50. *Providence Journal*, October 22, 1979.

51. Ibid., April 28, 1978.

52. Frazier Lang, telephone interview with author, December 1985.

53. *Bryant Review*, 1: 1 (Fall 1978), 1.

54. Office of Institutional Advancement. End of Year Financial Report for 1978–79.

CHAPTER 7

1. "College Mission," Report of the Long-Range Planning Committee, 1979.

2. William O'Hara, "A Season of Change for Bryant College," *Bryant Review* 7: 4: 12 (November 1984).

3. "Catalyst for Quality: The Report of the First Strategic Planning Committee." Bryant College, Smithfield, Rhode Island, September 1984.

4. Clarissa Patterson, written communication, August 1986.

5. Karl Ericson, interview with author, August 15, 1985, tape-recorded in Providence, Rhode Island, 1: 228.

6. Frank C. Pierson, et al., *The Education of American Businessmen* (New York: McGraw-Hill, 1959), 52.

7. Ericson, interview, 1: 270.

8. "Re-Evaluation Report. Prepared for the Commission on Institutions of Higher Education, New England Association of Colleges and Secondary Schools." Submitted by Bryant College, Providence, Rhode Island, April 1968.

9. Jo-Anne Lema, "Fact Book, 1984–85," Table 2, "All Applicants by Major, Percentage Change Over Five Years, 1977–81."

10. Wallace Wood, interview with author, December 1985.

11. Clarissa Patterson, interview with author, July 24, 1985, tape-recorded at Bryant College, 2: 541–687.

12. Henry Foley, interview with author, July 29, 1985, tape-recorded at Bryant College, 3: 396.

13. Quoted in "Profiting From the Humanities," by C. Ralph Adler, *Bryant Review*, November 1983, pp. 14–16.

14. *Bryant Review*, July 1981.

15. "The 'Face' of the Graduate School," *Bryant Review*, April 1983.

16. *Bryant Review*, April 1983.

17. *Journal Bulletin* (Providence), June 1, 1985, A-4.

18. Hinda Pollard, interview with author, December 9, 1985. Kathleen Simons, interview with author, December 9, 1985.

19. Pollard, interview.

20. *Bryant Review*, April 1983, p. 5.

21. Pollard, interview; Simons, interview.

22. Susan Sheplak, telephone conversation with author, December 16, 1985.

23. Sharon Gederman, telephone conversation with author, December 16, 1985.

24. David V. Kaiser, "An Analysis of My Cooperative Education Experience with the General Motors Corporation," December 1985, p. 37.

25. Pollard, interview.

26. Michael R. Poshall, "Learn While You Earn," *Ocean State Business*, August 19, 1985.

27. Rosemary D'Arcy, interview with author, August 1985; written communication, August 1986. See also John Louis Nero, *Business Fortnightly*, August 18, 1985, p. 19.

28. Raymond Fogarty, interview with author, August 1985; written communication, August 1986.

29. Ibid.

30. Edward Golden, interview with author, December 19, 1985.

31. Noreen Mattis, interview with author, December 19, 1985.

32. Robert Reall, interview with author, December 12, 1985.

33. John F. Gillooly, "Bryant Basketball History," 1985; Reall, interview.

34. *Bryant Review*, 4: 2 (April 1981), 1.

35. Debbie Turner, interview with author, December 18, 1985.

36. Elizabeth Covino, interview with author, December 12, 1985.

37. Fred S. Kenney, interview with author, December 12, 1985.

38. Ibid.

39. Bernard Blumenthal, interview with author, December 19, 1985.

40. Golden, interview.

41. Joseph A. Ilacqua, interview with author, December 17, 1985.

42. Alton Mott, private communication, January 30, 1987.

43. *Bryant Review*, November 1980.

44. Office of Institutional Advancement. End of Year Financial Report for 1979–80, 1980–81, 1983–84, 1984–85, 1985–86. (Archives of Institutional Advancement.)

45. William O'Hara, interview with author, August 8, 1985, tape-recorded at Bryant College, 1: 337.

46. Ibid., 2: 001.

143

BRYANT COLLEGE: *The First 125 Years*

was designed by Gilbert Associates and printed by Meridian Printing on Bowaters Gleneagle paper.

The type is Goudy Old Style, designed by Frederic W. Goudy in 1915.

The book has been bound by Zahrndt's, Inc.

5,000 copies were printed on the occasion of the 125th anniversary of Bryant College.

January, 1988